CLIMBERS
AND
WALL PLANTS
FOR
YEAR ROUND
COLOUR

CLIMBERS
AND
WALL PLANTS
FOR
YEAR ROUND
COLOUR

Jane Taylor

WARD LOCK

ACKNOWLEDGEMENTS

The publishers are grateful to the following for granting permission to reproduce the colour photographs:

Jane Taylor (pp. 14, 23, 27, 58, 62, 74, 79, 86/87 and 94); Harry Smith Horticultural Photographic Collection (pp. 2, 7, 15, 22, 26, 30/31, 35, 38, 39, 47, 55, 75, 86, 90, 91, 95 and 102); Photos Horticultural Picture Library (Cover: main and right-hand photographs; pp. 10/11, 11, 43, 46, 66, 78 and 107); Pat Brindley (pp. 19, 63, 67, 71 and 83); Elizabeth Whiting & Associates (Cover: left-hand photograph) and Richard Carr (p. 110).

The photographs on pp. 70 and 98 were taken by John Heseltine and Bob Challinor respectively

All the line drawings were drawn by Mike Shoebridge

First published in Great Britain in 1993
by Ward Lock Limited, Villiers House, 41/47 Strand,
London WC2N 5JE, England
A Cassell Imprint

© Jane Taylor 1993

Text filmset by RGM Associates, Southport

Printed and bound in Hong Kong

CIP data for this book is available upon application
from The British Library

ISBN 0 7063 7095 3

CONTENTS

	Preface	6
Chapter 1	Taking Stock: Winter	8
Chapter 2	The Garden Awakens: Spring	18
Chapter 3	A Burst of Colour and Scent: Early to Midsummer	37
Chapter 4	The Ripening Year: High to Late Summer	59
Chapter 5	The Nights Draw In: Autumn	82
Chapter 6	Cultivation	93
Appendices I	A Calendar of Colour from Climbers and Wall Plants	111
II	Climbers for Autumn and Winter Leaf Colour	118
III	Climbers and Wall Shrubs for Ornamental Fruit	119
IV	Climbers with Coloured or Variegated Foliage	120
V	Climbers Classified by Flower Colour	121
VI	Wall Plants Classified by Flower Colour	123
Bibliography		125
Index		126

PREFACE

NO GARDENER WHO AIMS for year-round colour can afford to ignore climbers. They add colour in the minimum of ground space, and can enhance or extend the season of a host tree or shrub, or transform a hedge, fence or outhouse. Even without special structures for their support – pergolas, arches, gazebos – most gardens could offer a home to many more climbers than their owners may realize.

Climbers can of course, pre-eminently, be grown on walls. On house walls they combine with a foundation planting of wall shrubs to link house and garden, making these two categories of plant among the most important design elements in the garden. Gardeners who are fortunate enough to have boundary walls as well will find climbers add another dimension to shrub and flower borders.

With the extra protection of a wall, many shrubs and climbers – especially evergreens – that might be tender in the open border can be made to thrive. Others, native to areas where the summers are hot and long, benefit from the extra ripening they gain on a sunny wall, to flower with greater abandon. Walls, therefore, allow us to widen the range of plants from which we can choose to add year-round colour.

There are also climbers and wall shrubs that will grow and flower in difficult, cold and exposed places. In the open garden, shrubs and climbers can be paired for maximum impact or seasonal succession from spring until autumn.

Not all climbers make permanent woody stems; some die to the ground in winter, and others can be grown like annuals from seed each year. These are especially useful for providing quick colour, and for ringing the changes year by year in borders, on walls and among the permanent occupants of pergolas and arches.

I have chosen to begin this book with a chapter on the garden in winter, for it is a time to take stock, to enjoy evergreens and the delicate, often sweetly fragrant flowers of the cold months. As the garden awakes in spring, early flowers open in the shelter of warm walls, and in every corner of the garden a climber could be decorating a host shrub or tree.

Spring gives way to summer, the opulence of colour and scent transforms the garden. Climbers on pergolas and rope swags, trees and fences, smothering outhouses and framing doors and windows add to the richness of the season.

Clematis cirrhosa balearica *needs a sheltered place to protect its delicate creamy bells from weather damage. They open during mild spells in winter.*

The year ripens into late summer, when climbers have a major role to play in keeping colour going in the garden. In sheltered sitting out places on patios and terraces, choice climbers and wall shrubs add to the ambience, and in the hottest places exotic climbers add a tropical note of colour and luxuriance.

As the nights draw in, the nostalgic season of autumn takes over, and the last flowers of summer reluctantly give way to the colours of fruit and dying foliage before, once again, it is time for winter and the stage is left to the evergreens.

J.T.

CHAPTER 1

TAKING STOCK
WINTER

SOME PEOPLE DREAD the cold weather. But like everything else in life, winter has its positive side as well. It's a time when you can take stock, making plans for the garden without feeling that you should be deadheading or watering or weeding. And it's a time, too, to enjoy the garden. Winter has much to offer in the way of interest, from the tracery of bare branches against the sky to the intimacy of the season's flowers, some of them intensely fragrant.

Many of the wall shrubs and climbers you grow will be on show twelve months of the year. It is worth, then, including a good proportion of evergreen foliage as well as winter flowers. It is easy to have plenty of flowers among the leafage of spring and summer, but winter won't take care of itself: you must plan for it in advance.

There's another advantage to choosing year-round or evergreen shrubs and climbers for the walls of your house. Foundation planting, as it is often called, is about integrating buildings and gardens, so that – seen from the outside – the house sits comfortably in its mini-landscape. Then there's the other way of looking at the garden: out from indoors. Creative foundation planting also ensures that the garden picture is framed by the shrubs and climbers around the windows.

Gardeners are often tempted by the shelter of a wall to grow plants on the borderline of hardiness. The shrubs and climbers you choose for your foundation plantings, however, should be reliably hardy, at least in a normal winter. Otherwise you may find yourself starting again from scratch even before your plants are properly established. Even in normal winters, the less hardy evergreens can look pinched or their leaves may become singed by frost, which will hardly contribute to your enjoyment of them at this season.

The ideal foundation shrub or climber is hardy, with handsome evergreen foliage and a bold or firm structure. It should grow in any reasonable soil and not require very damp conditions, which soil beside a wall will never provide. If it has good flowers in its season, that is a bonus to be enjoyed.

EVERGREEN FOLIAGE

Favourite climbers such as roses, clematis, honeysuckle, triumphant in their season, have nothing to offer in winter. A trachelospermum, or a variegated euonymus or ivy, on the other hand, always looks presentable. If you must have summer colour as well, you could run a clematis up through their branches or ring the changes with annual climbers.

I used to live near a house which was clad in variegated ivy, not just around the front door but over the whole façade. It was kept immaculately trimmed at the eaves and around the windows, and as a result this otherwise plain house always looked smart, yet not ostentatious. Ivy will stand any amount of clipping to keep it flat to the wall and contained within the space you intend for it.

Some say that ivy damages walls. But in my experience, a wall that is sound, whether of brick or stone, is at no risk. Indeed, the ivy helps to keep the house warm and dry. Against that, more than many other climbers, ivy does collect dust and dead foliage. Has anyone ever tried vacuum cleaning their ivy, I wonder?

Euonymus fortunei is apt to grow exuberantly outwards as well as upwards. This gives a more informal look than clipped ivy: the difference, say, between relaxed weekend wear and a tailored suit. There are several varieties of the euonymus, variegated in cream or gold, or plain green turning to mahogany and crimson in winter ('Coloratus'); and hundreds of different ivies, plain or fancy, large or small in leaf. Choose the one you like the look of, and ask about its vigour before you buy, to be sure you have picked one that will cover as much wall as you want. You can, of course, also grow them on tree trunks, old stumps and fences, on poles and pillars in your borders, or simply as ground cover.

All-seasons wall coverings

Pyracanthas (or firethorns), which I shall describe in more detail in Chapter 5, lend themselves very well to wall training, and they can easily reach the eaves of a two-storey house. In early summer their creamy flowerheads are attractive against the evergreen foliage, and the bright berries, yellow, orange or red, bring colour to the autumn and winter scene.

Decorative and reliable though they are, firethorns and ivies are perhaps just a touch plebeian. If you want something with a bit more distinction, and poignantly fragrant flowers too (in summer), choose one of the trachelospermums, evergreen climbers from Asia with half-twining, half-clinging stems. The shelter of a wall suits them well, in sun or – in warmer areas – half shade. Unusually, the cream-marbled *Trachelospermum jasminoides* 'Variegatum' is hardier than the plain green type (described in Chapter 4); it often turns to crimson-pink in winter, making it very much an all-seasons climber. If you dislike variegations, but still welcome rich winter tones, there is *T. jasminoides* Wilson 776, its bronzed leaves turning to crimson with the cold.

The hydrangea tribe, too – better known for seaside shrubs bearing blue or pink mopheads – offers a handful of evergreen, self-clinging climbers, with cream or ivory flowers. For year-round foliage, *Pileostegia viburnoides* probably

Above: *In winter the cream and green foliage of* Trachelospermum jasminoides *'Variegatum' takes on rich tones of pink and crimson.*

Left: *The dense evergreen foliage of* Euonymus fortunei *'Silver Queen' is enlivened by the cream markings on the leaves. Pink and white heathers give colour to this winter group.*

has the edge. It will grow in sun or shade, though it flowers more freely with plenty of light. Hardy and vigorous, reaching 6 m (20 ft), it has bold, long-oblong, deep green leaves to set off its wide heads of tiny ivory flowers in late summer. The rare *Decumaria sinensis* (Chapter 3) is almost as handsome in leaf. *Hydrangea serratifolia* (Chapter 4), like these, is self-clinging and evergreen.

The rampant honeysuckle *Lonicera japonica* is sometimes described as evergreen, but it cannot honestly be said to look like much in winter. However, some lesser-known honeysuckles are worth their place all year because of their luxuriant leafy covering. *Lonicera henryi* has slender-pointed, dark green leaves up to 10 cm (4 in) long, borne on vigorous growth; its flowers which open in summer are nothing to shout about. My choice, though, is *L. giraldii*, which is equally vigorous and has narrow leaves not much smaller, heart-shaped at the base, and thick with velvety down so that they are a joy to stroke. Again, the flowers are of the 'so-what' variety, small red-purple and yellowish confections in summer.

Climbers such as *Holboellia* and *Stauntonia* are grown more for their flowers than their leaves, and will receive due attention in Chapter 2. But they are evergreen, and they do have quite bold foliage that looks respectable all year unless caught by severe frost or icy winds.

Evergreen shrubs to furnish walls in winter

One of the classic wall coverings is *Garrya elliptica*, a large evergreen shrub which bears its catkin-like, grey-green flowers in winter on male plants. A selection with especially generous tassels is 'James Roof'. Although garryas will do as well on a sunless as on a sunny wall, and will stand exposure to sea winds, they dislike cold cutting winds. Less commonly seen, *G.* × *thuretii* has very large, glossy, dark green leaves up to 15 cm (6 in) long.

In cold climates the loquat, *Eriobotrya japonica*, seldom if ever bears fruit, but this can be turned to advantage if you decide to grow it purely as a foliage plant (Fig. 1). Fruiting specimens can look rather scrubby, but a loquat that is putting all its energies into its foliage is magnificent, with 30 cm (12 in) long, leathery, corrugated leaves. It deserves the shelter of a wall to keep them unmarked by frost or wind.

There are some flowering evergreen shrubs that also appreciate the shelter of a wall, and earn their keep by looking good even in winter, when out of flower. If you plant the Mexican orange blossom, *Choisya ternata* (Chapter 2), or *Viburnum japonicum* (Chapter 3) you will have a shrub that furnishes your walls twelve months of the year, with the bonus of fragrance to look forward to. The magnificent *Fatsia japonica* (Fig. 2), a shrubby relative of ivy, has huge, fingered leaves. You could set it against a wall where the shadows of its leaves will make dramatic patterns, or clothe the wall behind it with an ivy such as *Hedera colchica* 'Sulphur Heart', its leaves boldly splashed with creamy yellow.

Sometimes a smaller shrub may be what you need, paired either side of a doorway perhaps, or tucked in beneath a ground floor window. For a shady position, my choice among evergreen shrubs might be a skimmia such as *S.*

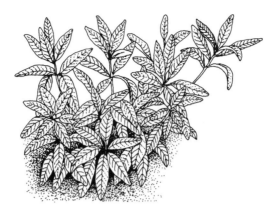

Fig. 1 Eriobotrya japonica *is grown for its fruits in warm-temperate to hot climates, but in cooler areas it makes a fine wall shrub with bold, handsome, evergreen foliage.*

japonica 'Fragrans' for its domed flowers, filling the air with lily-of-the-valley perfume in spring, or the wide-spreading *S.* × *confusa* 'Kew Green', so called for its heads of deliciously fragrant ivory-green flowers. *S. japonica* 'Rubella' has deep crimson flower buds during winter, opening in spring. They are more often grown in the open ground, or in containers ('Fragrans' is common in London window boxes), but could well be grown at the foot of a climber to mask its bare lower stems.

Fig. 2 *The large, palmate, polished leaves of* Fatsia japonica *look well in association with stone or against a whitewashed wall. It is a splendid town-garden plant and also grows well in a large tub.*

The white flowers of Camellia sasanqua *'Narumigata' open in winter, but have a spring-like freshness and fragrance.*

THE SCENTS OF WINTER

Winter is the season of the Japanese *Camellia sasanqua*, and its varieties. They are slightly tender, needing a sheltered wall in mild gardens, a conservatory or sunroom elsewhere. They also need plenty of sun, wherever their home, in order to flower freely. Try training one fan or espalier style on a sunny wall. All camellias dislike lime, but the sasanquas are the nearest to lime-tolerant, so a neutral soil suits them. Chalk, however, or soil contaminated with lime mortar and builder's rubble, is no good for them.

Given suitable soil and a warm sunny wall, you can expect smallish but sweetly fragrant flowers in late autumn and winter from your sasanquas. One of the most reliable is 'Narumigata', its single white flowers tipped with pink. Another old single-flowered variety is 'Crimson King'. 'Plantation Pink' has larger flowers than many. The sasanquas come with semi-double or double flowers as well, just like the *C. japonica* varieties.

Opposite: *The quiet colouring of* Garrya elliptica, *its silvery catkins hanging amid dark leaves, is in tune with winter's mood.*

The fragrant flowers of winter are seldom showy – the sasanqua the exception – but the sweetness is the more poignant on account of their modesty. One of the most retiring is *Azara microphylla*, an evergreen shrub that needs wall shelter in cold areas. With its slender, fanning branches and small, neat, dark green leaves, it makes a delicate pattern against stone or whitewash. The flowers, tiny puffs of yellow, hide on the reverse of the branches; but bend your nose to them, and you will find that, though barely visible, they give off a powerful aroma of vanilla custard.

I have struggled for years to find words for the fragrance of the wintersweet, *Chimonanthus praecox*. Sweet, slightly spicy, and sharp, it has an elusively evocative quality. Only the perfume of the winter-flowering narcissi such as 'Paper White' seems to me to bear any likeness to it. The fragrance is all in the flowers, their translucent petals stained with crimson at the centre. 'Grandiflorus', as its name suggests, has larger flowers; 'Luteus', though, would be my choice, for the petals are clear waxy lemon in colour. The shrub itself has a somewhat spicy, dusty aroma, most noticeable in the brown seed pods.

There are drawbacks, of course: the wintersweet is a rather coarse thing in leaf, and it takes several years to flower even when trained to a wall to catch all the ripening rays of the sun. But then you can always run a clematis or an annual climber through its branches to flower in summer and avoid having a plant, however treasured, which is of interest in only one season.

A big shrub, the wintersweet needs a fair expanse of wall. The winter-flowering *Daphne bholua* is more modest in growth, usually making a slender 1.8 m (6 ft) shrub; the richly fragrant white, pinkish or purple-flushed flowers are scarcely less discreet in looks than the wintersweet's. Since this daphne was introduced to the west from its native Himalayas it has won popularity and is available in different guises, from the more tender evergreen forms to the fully hardy ones from higher altitudes. In many ways these, which lose their leaves in winter, are preferable to the evergreens, as the little flower clusters show better on bare branches. They have the hint of clove and carnation in their scent that is often found in daphnes.

Another with similar flowers among evergreen leaves is *Daphne odora*, though it barely qualifies as a winter-flowering shrub unless the season is very mild. The form most people grow, because it is hardier, is called 'Aureomarginata', as its leaves are finely edged with creamy yellow. If you like variegations, keep an eye open for a newer kind (not yet in commerce as I write) with much bolder, brighter gold-edged leaves.

Fragrant shrubs for warm corners

If you have a very warm and sheltered wall, you could try one of the mimosas, or a winter-flowering buddleia. *Acacia dealbata* is one of the hardiest and easiest mimosas, the fluffy, fragrant yellow bobbles opening in late winter among feathery, grey-green foliage. If cut back by frost it generally grows away again from ground level. It is easy to raise from seed, and fast-growing, the kind of shrub worth experimenting with as you have little to lose if a hard winter does slaughter it.

Most buddleias are rather formless shrubs; but much can be forgiven a butterfly bush that flowers in winter. *Buddleja auriculata* has greyish foliage and spikes of deliciously fragrant, creamy flowers each enhanced by a yellow eye, borne on bare branches. Once established it will usually grow away from the roots even if cut to the ground by severe frost. The more tender *B. asiatica* has very long drooping tassels of sweetly perfumed ivory flowers among narrow, white-backed leaves. Both do best in full sun, on a very warm and sheltered wall.

Winter's climbers

Fragrance can be elusive, even to those with an acute sense of smell. In the case of *Clematis cirrhosa*, the delicate lemon scent of its understated, creamy-green bells is best experienced under cover. If you have a large enough plant, you can pick a strand or two and enjoy the flowers indoors. They certainly merit close inspection, and not just for their fragrance; some forms, notably one called 'Freckles', are marked with maroon inside the bells. 'Wisley Form', on the other hand, is pure primrose-cream. All have divided leaves that turn bronze in winter; variety *balearica* is ferny-fine in leaf.

Although it has no scent, the winter jasmine, *Jasminum nudiflorum*, remains ever popular for its cheery yellow flowers along green, leafless branches in winter. Pair it with an evergreen shrub such as *Mahonia aquifolium*, which takes on bronze tones in winter where the sun strikes it, or let it thread its way through a fishbone cotoneaster (*Cotoneaster horizontalis*) for a bright winter picture of yellow and red.

CHAPTER 2

THE GARDEN AWAKENS
SPRING

S PRING IS A CHALLENGING time in the garden. On the one hand, there is the thrill of awakening, the sense of resurgence as, responding to lengthening days and the return of warmth, plants burgeon. On the other, there may be the lurking threat of a treacherous frost or an icy, desiccating wind, capable in a moment of blackening those tender, budding leaves and flowers.

In some climates, such as that of north-eastern America, spring is a short hectic season that all too quickly surrenders to summer. In the more maritime climes of the western seaboard, of Britain and western Europe, spring may be long drawn out, coming in fits and starts. There may be a balmy spell when, to judge by the date, winter's grip should still be firm, followed – perhaps a month or more later – by the sudden reversion of spring to winter just as the gardener has come to believe that the frosts are finished.

Walls are the gardener's allies in the face of such challenges. They can provide shelter from wind and precious extra warmth for unfurling buds, as well as support.

COLD EXPOSED WALLS

Some walls, though, face the wrong way. They seem to catch all the biting winds and little or none of the sun. Even these walls, happily, can be made beautiful with climbers and shrubs.

Take, for instance, *Clematis montana*. Often grown on sunny walls or allowed to rampage through a host tree – a white montana looks stunning in a tall dark conifer, the pink forms charming in a grey-blue one – it will in fact grow where almost nothing else will. If you have a high, dark, cold wall, *Clematis montana* is your ally. It can reach as much as 12 m (40 ft), can be left virtually alone if you don't want to bother with pruning, and needs only to be kept out of the gutters. If you think your montana might grow too large for its space, you can prune it immediately after flowering each year. The alternative is to leave well alone until it actually gets out of hand, when you will cut the whole tangle of stems back, with some risk of killing the plant instead of rejuvenating it.

The natural colour of *C. montana* is white, though there are wild pink forms classed as *C. montana rubens*, of which the best are rosy mauve with the pigment tinting the foliage also to a bronze tone. Several garden varieties inherit this tendency, though in my experience the deeper pinks are less fragrant than the whites, or not fragrant at all. 'Picton's Variety' is one of the deepest in colour and least vigorous; like all the montanas, it is paler in shade (an unexpected characteristic, as we usually expect flowers to be bleached by the sun rather than the converse). 'Pink Perfection' is paler and nicely scented, while paler still is 'Vera', which is also fragrant. For colour, there is 'Freda', a cherry pink with bronzed foliage, and 'Rubens Superba' a good selection from the wild *rubens*. 'Mayleen' is a newish introduction with large deep pink flowers amid bronzed leaves. If you like size above all in your flowers, go for 'Tetrarose', which has been given a colchicine boost to double its chromosome count. The colour is a pleasant deep rosy mauve. One must not forget the variety 'Marjorie', which has

Osmanthus delavayi makes a bold mound of dark green foliage all year, transformed in spring when the countless tiny, fragrant white blooms open.

an extra row of creamy pink sepals around deeper pink stamens.

The most famous pink montana may be 'Elizabeth', on account of its vanilla fragrance as much as its fair-sized pale pink flowers, almost white if grown in a dark place. The pale pink 'Odorata', as its name suggests, is also fragrant. One of the finest whites is 'Alexander', with well-rounded, sizeable ivory flowers and a warm vanilla perfume. The whiteness of 'Grandiflora' is more declamatory, but the flowers have no scent. *C. montana sericea*, which you may also find listed as *C.* 'Spooneri', has downy foliage and large white flowers with no fragrance at all. At the end of the montana season comes *C. wilsonii*, a month after the rest, its white flowers endowed with a chocolate aroma.

Clematis among shrubs

Not all spring-flowering clematis are as rampant as *C. montana*. *C. alpina* or *C. macropetala* will also grow happily on a sunless wall; indeed, they look very well scrambling through some of the shrubs best suited to these same cold walls – flowering quinces in red, orange, coral or white, or kerria in yellow, combine in a picture of spring freshness with the clear kitten's eye blue of a clematis. There are several different blue *C. alpina* cultivars. 'Pamela Jackman' has rich blue flowers with broad petals; 'Frances Rivis' in clear mid blue has large flowers enhanced by white stamens. Paler again is 'Columbine', which has longer, more pointed sepals. One of the deepest in colour is 'Helsingborg', in rich purple-blue.

I like to see these blues with the paler coral or soft orange flowering quinces, such as *Chaenomeles speciosa* 'Phylis Moore' or *C.* × *superba* 'Yaegaki' or 'Coral Sea'. The brighter scarlet or rich blood red quinces look well with a white *Clematis alpina*, such as 'White Columbine', or the very free-flowering 'Burford White' which has pale, spring-fresh foliage. 'White Moth' is a later-flowering variety which might bloom too late to catch the quince. One of the most popular red quinces is *Chaenomeles* × *superba* 'Crimson and Gold' – the gold comes from its yellow anthers – but it can be rather a spreader. 'Knap Hill Scarlet' is a very fine, long-flowering orange-scarlet, and 'Rowallane' has large crimson red flowers. For a small space, under a low window perhaps, *C. speciosa* 'Simonii' is ideal; its very deep blood red flowers stand out vividly against a white wall or among the white lanterns of the clematis.

Either a blue or a white clematis would assort well with pink-flowering quinces such as *Chaenomeles speciosa* 'Moerloosii' in pale pink and white or the deeper *C.* × *superba* 'Pink Lady'. But when it comes to 'pink' *Clematis alpina*, beware: there is too much mauve in their colouring to blend with the clear tones of the quinces. 'Willy' in pale dusty pink is a good newer variety, but 'Rosy Pagoda' has a prettier name; and the old 'Ruby' has deeper, dusky mauve-pink flowers. If you want to stay with the quinces, they need to be paired with white *Chaenomeles speciosa* 'Snow' or 'Nivalis'.

Much the same mauvy tones belong to the 'pink' *Clematis macropetala*, 'Markham's Pink' and to the more recent 'Rosie O'Grady'. I want to recommend, not for the first time, a planting of 'Markham's Pink' with the cupped, chocolate-maroon, spice-scented flowers of *Akebia quinata*, which also does well on a shady wall. This combination enhances two climbers that are not always easy to place to their best advantage; their colours, both muted, complement each other when they could easily be cancelled out in the wrong setting. To my eye – and these things are very personal, of course – it works far better than the famous combination of blue and pink *C. macropetala* in the Ali Baba jar at Sissinghurst Castle gardens in Kent, southern England, the creation of Vita Sackville-West.

Clematis macropetala has fuller flowers than *C. alpina*, the extra sepals giving it the look of a flower wearing several petticoats. 'Blue Lagoon' (syn. 'Maidwell Hall') and 'Blue Bird' are good blue selections, and in white there are 'White Swan' and the later-flowering 'Snowbird' to choose from.

Yellow and blue, especially in the softer ranges of the two colours, always look well together. *Kerria japonica* is a tough, spring-flowering shrub perfectly happy on a sunless wall (or indeed in an open border). The most familiar kerria is the double 'Pleniflora', which bears cheerful ragged pompoms of bright yolk yellow. Less showy but more refined, 'Golden Guinea' has large, clear yellow, single flowers. It's all a matter of taste which you prefer, but either will create a perfect spring picture if planted with *Clematis alpina* or *C. macropetala* in any of their pretty blue varieties mentioned above.

Earlier in the year, *Forsythia suspensa* bears its clear yellow flowers on long lax stems, ideal for training to a wall, where it can easily reach the eaves of a two-storey house. Though less assertive in flower than the familiar *Forsythia × intermedia* 'Spectabilis', it is welcome for its early colour and for its willingness to flower on a sunless wall. Two forms, *atrocaulis* and 'Nymans', have bronze-black stems contrasting with the lemon-primrose flowers.

SHELTERED PLACES FOR EARLY FLOWERS

Other things being equal, houses have more than one wall, and if one is cold and exposed, at least one other should be warm and sheltered, or capable of being made so. Walls that face right into the midday sun are the most suitable for plants that need all the sun they can get to ripen their wood so as to flower well. Walls that face the afternoon sun are an ideal home for many plants that need a little encouragement, either to protect their flowers from frost or to provide extra warmth to help them through the winter. A wall that faces the levant is less congenial; it has all afternoon to lose heat once the sun has moved on, while the wall facing the setting sun gains the benefit of the rays at their warmest.

Making the most of warm walls

In order to exploit all the potential of your walls, you may need to ensure that the heat they retain is not dissipated by wind. A fence, a series of living buttresses along the wall, even a temporary screen of proprietary windbreak material, can all help to cut the wind and save a few precious degrees of heat. Evergreen shrubs that stand clipping, such as *Pittosporum tenuifolium*, make good buttresses where the climate is not too severe, with in this case the bonus of chocolate-scented, maroon flowers in spring.

For a sheltered wall, the pure white Clematis indivisa *is even more dramatic than the tough and hardy* C. montana.

The Mexican orange blossom, *Choisya ternata*, has aromatic, glossy, dark green leaves formed of three blunt-ended leaflets, and starry, white, fragrant flowers in spring and early summer. It will do equally well in sun or shade. With its rounded outline, it looks well filling the angle between two walls, or it can provide shelter for more tender wall shrubs and climbers. Its golden form, 'Sundance', is slower growing; the vivid leaves make a striking contrast with a blue *Clematis alpina*. A newer, hybrid choisya called 'Aztec Pearl' (Fig. 3) has slender-fingered, dark green leaves and clusters of ivory, yellow-eyed flowers in spring, contributing to an elegant shrub that seems just as easy-going as the more familiar *C. ternata*.

Osmanthus delavayi, a Chinese native that grows slowly to 2 m (7 ft), is another hardy evergreen shrub that could be grown on a wall both for its own qualities

Opposite: *A spring pairing of* Forsythia suspensa *with* Clematis alpina *mixes near-blue and soft yellow in a classic colour scheme.*

Fig. 3 *Less familiar than the Mexican orange,* Choisya *'Aztec Pearl' has elegant, slim-fingered, evergreen leaves and ivory flowers enlivened by golden stamens in spring.*

and to help shelter more tender plants. Its small neat leaves are very dark green, and set off clusters of tiny, pure white flowers endowed with a strong sweet perfume when they open in spring.

Camellias on walls

With some shrubs, such as camellias, wall shelter is often desirable to protect the flowers, even in areas where the plant itself is hardy. *Camellia japonica*, when first introduced to the west, was grown in hothouses, but before long growers found that it would stand several degrees of frost without damage. Even the more tender *C. reticulata* is able to stand some frost, and some of its hybrids are very weather-resistant. *C. japonica* and others need less sun, on the whole, than the winter-flowering *C. sasanqua*, flowering freely even on a sunless wall so long as there is plenty of overhead light. However, a wall that faces the morning sun is less suitable. It used to be said the reason was that the sun, striking flowers still frosted from the night's chill, would cause them to thaw too fast, resulting in brown, damaged petals. Now camellia experts are denying this; but pragmatic gardeners prefer their camellia flowers to be unblemished, and are likely to go on avoiding walls the sun reaches too early.

Remember that for all camellias, the spring-flowering kinds even more than for the sasanquas, you need a soil free from lime. If the soil at the foot of your wall has been contaminated with builder's rubble, you will need to dig it out and replace it with something more suitable. The other requirement of camellias is plenty of water during summer when the flower buds are forming. Certain growers, it is true, have found their camellias coping well with dry summers, but it would be a pity to forgo the next season's flowers for the sake of a good soaking in summer.

The best camellias to grow on walls are those of rather lax growth that can be trained, or neat upright growers to fit into a small space, such as between a door and a window. The choice is wide, from the simplicity of *C. × williamsii* 'J.C. Williams' in dog-rose pink – especially suitable for a sunless wall – to the flounces and frills of *C.* 'Francie L', a *reticulata* hybrid but tough with it, its very large, rich rose pink flowers apparently immune to rough weather. The trio 'Dream Girl', 'Flower Girl' and 'Show Girl' also have *C. reticulata* blood; all are in shades of pink and flower very early in the season. On mild damp days you may catch their perfume, which is very noticeable when they are grown under glass. Another opulent pink is 'Mary Phoebe Taylor', which has graceful spreading branches.

'Elegant Beauty' does well on a shaded wall, where its deep pink, full flowers last well. The young growths are copper-tinted, as are those of 'Cornish Snow', an enchanting early flowering white single with slender branches. Others of stiffer growth, which do better as free-standing bushes against a shaded wall, include the deep pink single *C. × williamsii* 'St Ewe', and bell-shaped, hose-in-hose pink 'Bow Bells'. 'Inspiration' is a fine semi-double pink, long-lasting if given wall shelter, and 'Debbie' has peony-form, rose pink flowers over a very long season.

Californian lilacs

Ceanothus, being natives of California (though lilacs they are not), dislike extremes of cold, and are often grown on walls as a result. They need well-drained, neutral soil and a sheltered position in the sun. Many have quite attractive evergreen foliage, but it is above all their blue flowers which endear them to us. There are many to choose from, some better suited to growing on walls than others. Of the taller evergreen kinds, *Ceanothus impressus* reaches 2.5 m (8 ft) or more on a wall, and has exceptionally neat foliage, the tiny dark leaves marked with the deeply grooved veins that *impressus* describes. The spring flowers are deep ultramarine blue. 'Puget Blue' is another fine selection. One of the tallest is *C. arboreus* 'Trewithen Blue', rather coarse in leaf but very fine when bearing, in early spring, its large panicles of deep blue flowers.

The foliage of *Ceanothus dentatus* is much neater, and its flowers are bright blue. Its hybrids, *C. × lobbianus* 'Southmead', and the rather similar *C. × veitchianus*, both flower on into early summer. *C.* 'Italian Skies' is a splendid thing with vivid blue flowers in dense clusters; 'Delight' has long spikes of deep blue, and 'Cascade' is tall, with powder blue flowers on arching branches.

Rich blue belongs to *C. papillosus roweanus*, which has long, narrow, varnished leaves. It is much more compact, at 90–120 cm (3–4 ft), ideal for masking the lower limbs of a leggy clematis or large-flowered rose. 'Concha' flowers a little later, in bright cornflower blue. There are many others, both short and tall; almost all tend to billow forward with age, and resent hard pruning, so it's best to avoid planting them in a narrow wall bed.

Variety in the pea family

A seasonal splash of yellow can be provided on sheltered walls by the southern hemisphere sophoras – shrubs and small trees with tubular pea flowers which betray their origins. *Sophora microphylla* (Fig. 4) comes from Chile, an evergreen shrub with leaves composed of many small leaflets, and clusters of quite large, bright flowers in spring. The New Zealand kowhai, *S. tetraptera*, has even more delicate foliage, and hanging clusters of flowers in spring followed by seed pods like strings of brown beads. The daintiest leaves of all belong to *S. microphylla*,

Opposite: *One of the most dramatic viburnums is* V. macrocephalum, *which bears its great white snowballs in spring.*

Below: *Except for its season, you might think the shrubby* Olearia stellulata *was a very fine white Michaelmas daisy.*

slightly smaller in flower. In its juvenile stage it forms a tangled mass of stems, later developing into a shrub or small tree. All the sophoras prefer full sun and a sheltered wall, unless the climate is very mild.

Mimosas, too, belong to the pea family, though you would hardly know it, so different are their fluffy bobbles or slender spikes of yellow from the flowers of the sophoras, or of the brooms and coronillas that I shall describe shortly. There are many of these acacias, most of them needing wall shelter even in climates where the winters are mild but not frost free (in areas of severe winters they must be grown under glass). Here I want to pick out just two, one at least very easily raised from seed. *Acacia baileyana* has intensely blue, feathery-fine foliage, and sprays of yellow flowers in late winter and spring. It has a purple-leaved form, 'Purpurea', which comes more or less true from seed – pick out the darkest to grow on. It grows fast, so that even if a cold winter does it in, you are likely to have at worst a season's enjoyment of its dainty foliage for your pains.

The other, *Acacia pravissima*, has foliage of similar glaucous-blue brightness, but constructed quite differently, being formed of little triangular phyllodes (some acacias don't have leaves like other plants, but modified stems) strung edgeways, densely along the slender branches. The little yellow bobbles are gathered into long sprays and open in spring.

The brooms look more like what one expects from the pea family, with their keeled, winged flowers. In mild areas the florist's genista, *Cytisus canariensis*, will

Fig. 4 Sophora microphylla *bears showy, ochre-yellow flowers, and is equally decorative in foliage, each leaf composed of many tiny leaflets no bigger than beads.*

grow and flower on a warm sunny wall, producing its fragrant yellow flowers in spring. The Montpellier broom, *C. monspessulanus*, also merits wall space, and its offspring 'Porlock' is a fast-growing, leafy shrub with very fragrant yellow flowers in spring. If all this yellow is too much for you, try *Cytisus proliferus* from Tenerife, a small, half-weeping tree with ivory white flowers in spring, or *Genista monosperma*, a small shrub reaching 90 cm (3 ft) and bearing its sweet-scented white flowers in early spring.

The coronillas are relatives of the brooms, with fragrant yellow pea flowers and blue-green leaves. *Coronilla glauca* is the larger of the two; it has a form with pale lemon flowers called 'Citrina', and another, 'Variegata', with the leaves splashed cream – pale and pretty even without its canary yellow flowers. Both this and the more compact *C. valentina*, which smells like apricots, flower most abundantly in spring but are apt to show bloom at almost any time, including winter if the weather is very mild.

Leaf and blossom

The spring-flowering azaras are much less discreet than their winter-flowering cousin, *Azara microphylla*. *A. lanceolata*, a medium-sized shrub, has elegant, narrow, shining green leaves and bears quantities of bright yellow, fragrant flowers in spring. The azara season carries on into summer with *A. dentata* and *A. serrata*, both larger in leaf and quite showy in yellow, powder-puff flower.

For something much bolder in leaf, there is *Drimys winteri*, the winter bark, which I have seen used to great effect on a sheltered wall. In both foliage and flower it is handsome, the leaves often glaucous-white beneath, the fragrant ivory flowers opening in late spring. However, it is variable in habit, and the larger-growing forms need plenty of space. *D. w. andina* is compact and shrubby, flowering freely when still small.

One of the most striking wall shrubs for spring, in flower if not in leaf, is *Viburnum macrocephalum*. Semi-evergreen at best, it grows into a rounded shrub of about 1.8 m (6 ft), and bears in late spring great rounded heads, up to 15 cm (6 in) across, of white flowers.

Another shrub that appreciates wall shelter, this time to protect its early spring flowers, is *Prunus triloba*. The large double pompom flowers are clear peach pink. On a wall it is best pruned immediately after the blossom fades, by cutting back the flowered shoots.

The magnolia family, in spring, is mainly represented by trees and shrubs bearing pink or white flowers on bare branches. Closely related are the michelias, evergreen shrubs needing a mild climate and lime-free soil. If you can supply these, they are well worth planting for their powerfully fragrant flowers. *Michelia doltsopa*, in the right conditions, can make a small tree, with half-evergreen, leathery leaves up to 15 cm (6 in) long, glaucous beneath, and carrying

Overleaf: Clematis montana *is one of the most accommodating of spring climbers, growing with equal abandon in dark or sunny places.*

many-petalled white flowers which open from tawny-furred buds that form in autumn. 'Silver Cloud' is a selection with bright golden buds and larger, creamy flowers. *M. figo* has small, glossy leaves that are retained throughout the year and flowers that earn their keep not by their looks – they are comparatively dingy, brown-purple affairs – but by their amazing aroma of pear drops and ripe bananas.

Soft-toned flowers for spring

Following on from the winter-flowering buddleias, there are at least two spring-flowering species worth giving sunny wall space to. *Buddleia caryopteridi-folia* has white woolly leaves and sweetly scented, lilac flowers in late spring on the old wood (though it may also flower in autumn). More imposing than this is *B. farreri*, a tall shrub with handsome, velvety foliage backed with white wool, and fragrant mauve flowers in spring.

If you want to stay with the colour theme set by these buddleias but need a smaller, neater shrub, you could plant *Prostanthera rotundifolia*, the Australian mint bush. A small shrub with tiny aromatic leaves, it is covered in spring with a mass of lavender blue flowers, matching the daisies of *Olearia phlogopappa* 'Comber's Blue'. Both come in pink also – a pink that is near to mauve – so that you could match *Prostanthera rotundifolia* 'Rosea' with *Olearia phlogopappa* 'Comber's Pink'. *Prostanthera* 'Chelsea Pink' is also more mauve than pink, while *P. melissifolia* var. *parvifolia* is clear mauve, with larger flowers than *P. rotundifolia*. *Olearia stellulata*, greyish in leaf like all this group of daisy bushes, brings a note of startling whiteness to spring with its massed snowy heads of daisies.

These daisy bushes and mint bushes are small enough to tuck in around the feet of your climbers rather than elbowing them out. Larger and hardier than these, but still worth a place on a sunny wall especially in cold climates, *Ribes speciosum* is a refined shrub with glossy foliage, bristly, reddish stems, and hanging clusters of narrowly tubular, rich scarlet-crimson flowers in spring. It grows to about 1.8 m (6 ft). A warm, sunny spot suits *Rhaphiolepis × delacourii*, a slow-growing evergreen shrub that will eventually reach 1.8 m (6 ft). The sprays of bright pink flowers open in spring and summer against shining green leaves. 'Coates Crimson' is deeper rosy red in colour, and 'Spring Song', which has a longer season than its name implies, is apple-blossom pink.

Another, much more tender small shrub that brings a vivid touch to late spring is *Cantua buxifolia* (Fig. 5). The satiny, tubular flowers are bright cherry magenta with a touch of orange at the tips.

Spring-flowering climbers on warm sunny walls

Several evergreen climbers needing a warm, sheltered position flower in spring. *Clematis armandii* is a popular choice, both for its warm vanilla fragrance and for its bold, narrowly oblong, gleaming foliage, bronze-tinted when young. During cold winters, it's true, that foliage may be singed by frost so that it looks tatty rather than handsome; and unless you choose a named form, you may find

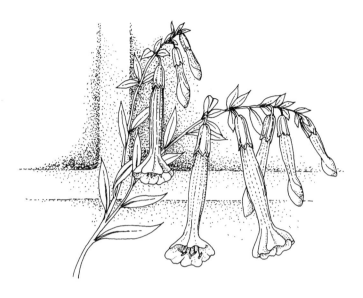

Fig. 5 *The frost-tender* Cantua buxifolia *has tubular, flared-mouthed flowers of daring magenta touched with yellow, in late spring.*

you have small dingy flowers instead of the generous clusters of white or blush pink you hoped for. 'Snowdrift' and 'Apple Blossom' are the two names to look out for; expect to pay more than for plain *C. armandii*, for they must be increased vegetatively, while the unadorned version might be a cheap, unpredictable seedling. Whether pedigree or not, *C. armandii* can take up a lot of space if it likes you; be prepared to trim it back after flowering unless you can allow it to shoot up to 9 m (30 ft) or more. Annual pruning keeps it tidy and free (or freer, at least) of old, bruised foliage.

More restrained in growth, the New Zealand *Clematis indivisa* has brilliant white flowers in abundance in spring, the effect rather like a very superior *C. montana*. By comparison, its fellow antipodean *C. forsteri* is shy and retiring; its lime yellow flowers, which are lemon-scented, are fresh and pretty among evergreen, divided leaves.

Many of the climbing jasmines are white-flowered, and earn a place in our hearts on account of their swooning perfume. The spring-flowering *Jasminum mesnyi* or primrose jasmine, though it does nothing for our sense of smell, delights the eye with its clear yellow, wide, semi-double flowers borne from early to late spring among evergreen foliage on growth of up to 4.5 m (15 ft). It needs a warm sunny position, and is one of the joys of little courtyard gardens in southern Europe.

The perfume of *Holboellia latifolia* is generous compensation for its half-hidden, green or dull brown flowers. Shelter, rather than full sun, is the recipe for success with this energetic evergreen climber, which has polished leathery foliage composed of three to seven leaflets. It flowers in early to mid spring and is followed a week or fortnight later by the very similar *H. coriacea*, which can also reach 6 m (20 ft) or more. Another related and very similar evergreen climber is *Stauntonia hexaphylla*, which has purple-washed white, fragrant flowers in spring and bold deep green foliage. All three, where the summers are hot and sunny, produce sausage-like purple fruits filled with seeds in pulpy, edible flesh.

Evergreen climbers like these and *C. armandii* can be used to host annual, summer-flowering climbers if you feel that their foliage is not sufficiently handsome to warrant all that wall space to themselves. That can give you scope for either continuing or varying your colour schemes through the season. The white bells of *Cobaea scandens* 'Alba', for example, stand out against the deep green summer foliage of these climbers.

Early roses on warm walls

In mild climates, such as that of the Mediterranean or much of California, the Banksian roses can be grown away from walls, filling a tree or simply sprawling into a wide bush. Where the winters are frosty, however, they need the shelter of a warm wall. They are among the first roses to flower, bearing their clusters of many small blossoms in spring, in white or yellow, single or double. The double yellow *Rosa banksiae* 'Lutea' is the most popular, and certainly the prettiest, its soft primrose yellow blooms making a fresh picture with the apple green foliage and green stems. Sadly, it is less fragrant than the single yellow *R. banksiae lutescens* or single white *R. banksiae normalis*. *R. banksiae banksiae*, which makes up the quartet, has full-petalled white flowers like tiny rosettes, well endowed with a sweet violet perfume. They are all generous in growth where the climate suits them. There is a hybrid of the Banksian rose, *R. × fortuneana*, with larger, double, ivory-cream flowers; it needs plenty of sun to flower freely.

Bridging the season between spring and summer are the Cherokee rose and its hybrids. *Rosa laevigata*, despite its common name, is a native of China, but has naturalized itself in the southern United States, and is the State flower of Georgia. On a warm wall it retains its polished, dark green leaves; the flowers are large, single and beautifully formed with creamy white petals and golden stamens, but they do not last long. Its hybrid 'Anemone' is better value in flower, the single clear pink blooms with paler reverse first opening early in the season and appearing over several weeks. 'Ramona' has the same elegantly formed flowers, but of deeper colouring – deep cerise pink with satiny buff reverse. Neither of these, though, can compare with their parent in leaf, and their growth is rather awkward.

PAIRING SHRUBS AND CLIMBERS

Already in this chapter I have suggested some combinations of shrubs and climbers – notably *Clematis alpina* and flowering quince or kerria, growing on a shady wall. The same effect of blue and yellow could be achieved on a warm, sunny wall by combining *Rosa banksiae* 'Lutea' with an evergreen ceanothus.

As spring passes into early summer, the richly coloured rose 'Ramona' opens the first of its wide, silky blooms.

But climbers, of course, do not have to be grown on walls. I have seen the yellow Banksian rose trained through wrought-iron railings in company with a ceanothus, both flowering madly in mid-spring in a sheltered town garden. In a cooler or shadier spot, you could equally well grow your *C. alpina* through a shrub such as *Physocarpus opulifolius* 'Dart's Gold', which has bronze-tinted yellow foliage, or *Pieris formosa forrestii* 'Wakehurst' with its brilliant red sprint shoots. The tree paeony, *Paeonia lutea ludlowii*, is another fine host for a blue alpine clematis, and a handsome plant in leaf even after its yellow, cupped flowers have faded.

In something bigger, such as a flowering thorn, you could grow a *Clematis montana* – white with a pink or red thorn, pink among white. Matching pink with pink doesn't work in this case, nor is it a good idea to grow *C. montana* in an old apple tree, because the clematis flowers are simply lost among the blossom. Choose a red-flowered, purple-leaved crab, though, and the clematis, whether white or pink, would stand out well against its dark background. *C. montana* can look stunning in the arms of a laburnum too; white and yellow, the epitome of spring. You would need to restrain the clematis to save the laburnum from being engulfed in time. You get an entirely different effect from growing your montanas up through a conifer. The happiest pairings are white *C. montana* in a dark cypress or yew, and the pink montanas in conifers of blue-grey tones. On a smaller scale, you could grow a white *C. alpina* over a dark, spreading juniper, or one of the blues sprawling through a golden juniper. Again, if you favour the dusky shades of pink *C. alpina* cultivars, a grey or bluish juniper would be your best choice for a low, spreading host conifer.

If you have a favourite colour scheme in spring that you would like to prolong into summer, but do not have the space for another shrub or perennial planting, climbers are your allies. It might be the fool simplicity of a white bridal wreath (*Spiraea arguta*) against the almost black-green of a yew, into whose branches you would train the viticella clematis hybrid 'Alba Luxurians' for summer white-on-green. The combination of *Berberis darwinii* with *Clematis alpina*, flame-orange and blue, would be picked up later in summer if the berberis – a large shrub at maturity – were to host orange-flowered *Eccremocarpus scaber* and a blue summer-flowering clematis, or even perhaps an azure-blue morning glory. Two climbers in one host shrub need not be a problem, especially if – as in the case of the eccremocarpus and morning glory – the twining stems die down in winter, leaving the evergreen host unencumbered. Several annual and herbaceous climbers of this kind are described in Chapter 4.

If both the host and its accompanying climber are grown for their flowers, there is no need for their season to coincide. Equally important is to look critically at your spring-flowering shrubs, asking each one – or yourself, if you are not keen on talking to your plants – how it would look with a climber in its branches to prolong its season. It is a characteristic of many popular spring shrubs that, once their blossom is over, they are boring in leaf. Think of forsythia, lilac, spiraea, flowering currant, and you'll see what I mean. In the chapters that follow you will find described plenty of climbers that you could grow through the branches of those old favourites to transform your garden in summer. The same principle works in reverse: a spring-flowering climber can enliven a summer-flowering shrub during the build-up to its own season.

I have recounted elsewhere how, only five years after starting to create a garden on a completely bare patch of ground, I decided to grow more climbers. Even in so new a garden, I found I had more potential hosts than I could afford to buy climbers for. In a mature garden, where you may think you have no space left for another plant, pairing shrubs and climbers with different seasons can give you double or triple the value from each patch of ground: more flower, more fragrance, more opportunities to combine colour and form in exciting new ways without having to rip out half your existing plants.

CHAPTER 3

A BURST OF
COLOUR AND SCENT
EARLY TO MIDSUMMER

FROM EARLY SUMMER for two months or more, a garden where climbers grow should be full of fragrance, as roses, honeysuckles, wisteria and jasmine come into flower; and full of colour, too, from large-flowered clematis and other scentless but treasured blooms. It is a generous season, yet it retains some of the freshness of spring and has still to develop into the opulence of late summer.

In summer, the structures that gardeners build for their climbers come into their own. Pergolas, rope swags, arches, trellis: these are some of the supports that not only enable us to grow more of our favourite climbers, but also form an important part of garden design. It is worth giving careful thought before you spend good money on artificial supports for your climbers. In an informal garden, they will almost always look incongruous, except perhaps near the house; you will do better to grow your roses and honeysuckles in a relaxed way, through and among host trees and shrubs. The more formal your garden layout, the more acceptable are man-made structures.

Pergolas, rope swags and arches

The original purpose of a pergola was not only to provide support for, typically, a vine, but also to make grateful shade where garden owners and their guests could seek refuge from the burning sun. The classic pergola with cross beams and a lattice of foliage overhead does not translate well to cooler, damper climates, where instead of enjoying the shade you may get an unwelcome shower down the back of your neck from rain-sodden foliage. To a lesser extent, an arch creates the same problem. From the design point of view, arches are best used to line a path or mark a change of direction, so that you are likely to find yourself frequently walking beneath them. If wet weather is what you most often have to contend with, consider instead a trellis, rope swag or succession of pyramids, which will provide as much space for your climbers without giving them the chance to grow overhead.

The other failing of a pergola is that if you use it to grow roses or clematis, most of the flowers will appear on the upper side of the crossbeams, and walking beneath you will scarcely see them. Vines are fine, as the bunches of grapes hang down, and wisteria bears hanging trails of flower too; but that's about it. Growing your climbers in one less dimension – upwards and sideways, but not crossways as well – means more of the flowers are borne where you can enjoy them.

THE CHOICE IN WISTERIAS

Whether you grow it on a pergola or over an arch, on a wall or into a large tree, or painstakingly train it into a standard tree, wisteria is one of the indispensable climbers of late spring and early summer. In those courtyard gardens of southern Europe where the primrose jasmine flowers from the earliest months of the year, the wisteria follows on with a tremendous display, encouraged by the hot sun of summer. A wisteria that does not flower is not worth its space; the foliage,

Wisteria's cascades of lilac tresses are beautifully displayed on this pergola, covering both the uprights and the cross beams.

though not objectionable, is certainly not justification enough. A combination of full sun, regular spurring back in both summer and winter, and the strictest abstinence from nitrogen-rich fertilizers, should ensure that your wisteria flowers abundantly, at least once it has got past its first youthful exuberance.

The colour range of wisteria is narrow but harmonious: lilac-mauve, a deeper purple-mauve, white, and pink leaning towards mauve. The Chinese *Wisteria sinensis* is distinguished from the Japanese *W. floribunda* when out of flower by the direction in which the stems twine: the Chinese plant twists anti-clockwise, the Japanese clockwise. In bloom, they are distinct in that the individual flowers of the Japanese open successively from the stem end to the tip, whereas on the flowering tassels of *W. sinensis* all the little pea flowers open more or less simultaneously.

The warm beanfield fragrance is fainter in *W. floribunda*. However, this species does offer one variety in which the tassels are very long, commonly 90 cm (3 ft) and occasionally up to twice as long, compared with the usual 25 cm (10 in) for the Japanese species or 30 cm (12 in) for the Chinese. This spectacular variety, 'Multijuga', needs to be grown where the long trails can hang free, so a pergola

The fragrant musk roses can be grown informally in trees or, as here, allowed to wreathe a gazebo in romantic profusion.

suits it well. On a wall, it needs very careful training to display the tassels at their best. Their colour is lilac with tinges of purple-blue.

There is a white *W. floribunda*, 'Alba', with racemes up to 60 cm (2 ft) long, while 'Snow Showers' is a newer white form. *W. f.* 'Rosea' was the first of the pinks, its colour leaning distinctly towards mauve, for the standards are pale pink and the keel violet. 'Peaches and Cream' has pink buds opening to white flowers, and 'Pink Ice' is a cleaner pink than 'Rosea'. 'Purple Patches' describes itself, while 'Violacea Plena', as its name implies, has double, lilac-blue flowers.

Even the Japanese wisteria needs plenty of room, as it can grow to 9 m (30 ft), but the Chinese plant can reach gigantic proportions of 30 m (100 ft), filling a tall tree or swamping a building if given the chance. The warm fragrance is especially marked in white *W. s.* 'Alba', and the newer 'Caroline' looks very promising with its deep blue-purple flowers and strong fragrance. 'Prematura', in lilac, and white 'Prematura Alba', are varieties selected for their quality of flowering from an early age, and 'Prolific' is said to live up to its name in the quantity of lilac flowers it bears.

Crosses between the Japanese and the Chinese wisterias include 'Issai', with rather short trails of blue-lilac flowers borne even on young shoots, and the double, deep purple 'Black Dragon'. One of the most beautiful of wisterias, with a warm fragrance, is the white *W. venusta*. The individual ivory-white flowers are large and borne in short but lasting racemes in early summer on growth to 9 m (30 ft).

The soft tones of lilac-mauve wisteria assort well with the tender yellow of early shrub roses such as *Rosa hugonis*, or – climate and space permitting – with the yellow Banksian rose. As the season moves on from early to midsummer, more and more roses come into their own, among them some of the most generous in both bloom and fragrance, to hold the stage as the wisterias fade.

FESTOONS OF ROSES

There are two kinds of roses that belong on pergolas, arches, rope swags and similar constructions. On the one hand, there are the generous, flexible-stemmed rambling or climbing roses that will festoon the cross-beams or enwreath the ropes that link your pillars: these are the ones I shall describe in this section. The shorter, stiffer varieties that belong on the pillars and uprights themselves are dealt with on page 65. From both, if you choose carefully, you can expect both fragrance and colour. Roses that are not fragrant, in my view, must have something else special to offer, perhaps an unusual colour, if they are to be worth growing.

A continuum of colour

Let's say you decide to keep the lilac and mauve theme of wisteria going well into the summer. Surprisingly, there are rambling roses dating from the early part of the twentieth century with lilac to purple flowers, at least as near to blue as the so-called blue large-flowered bush roses of more recent times. The first to open is 'Veilchenblau', the only one that adds scent to its qualities. The smallish blooms, held in clusters, are magenta purple streaked with white, fading to parma violet and lilac. Next comes 'Violette', which has more crimson in its colouring, retaining touches of maroon as it fades towards lilac-mauve.

Soon after this the first flowers of 'Rose-Marie Viaud' open to show their crimson and purple colouring, fading to soft violet and lilac. Like 'Veilchenblau' it has fresh light green foliage, and – like 'Violette' – the further advantage of almost thornless stems. The last of the quartet to bloom is 'Bleu Magenta', which has the largest flowers of the four: deep violet purple fading to grey-violet. They are all of comparable vigour, reaching 4–4.5 m (13–15 ft), and are well suited to growing on arches or rope swags. Another, only slightly less blue in colouring, is the much older and now uncommon 'Amadis', which flowers even before 'Veilchenblau'. Its scentless, cupped, semi-double crimson-purple flowers are borne on thornless stems. 'Russelliana' is another old rambler with small, clustered flowers of crimson colouring fading towards magenta with hints of purple; the stems are thorny but it compensates with its old rose perfume. The dusty miller vine, *Vitis vinifera* 'Incana', with its greyish leaf tones, assorts well with these roses.

Graceful rambling roses

One of the most graceful of ramblers is 'Adélaïde d'Orléans', a survivor from the early years of the nineteenth century. It has one generous midsummer season, and continues to be valued for its rosy buds opening to soft pink flowers with a delicate fragrance. Uniquely, they are held in hanging clusters, so that when this rose is grown on an arch or pergola the flowers nod towards you. Another pretty old rambler with a sweet fragrance, 'Blush Rambler' has soft pink, semi-double flowers on almost thornless stems reaching 4.5 m (15 ft).

'Evangeline', too, has a delicious fragrance; the pale pink flowers are single, giving a very dainty effect. Its crimson, white-eyed counterpart 'Hiawatha' has no scent, and bright pink 'Minnehaha' has almost none. These last two are paired rather by their names than their looks: 'Minnehaha' is more like a later, brighter version of the famous Edwardian rambler 'Dorothy Perkins'. Brighter still is 'Excelsa' in clear crimson; to keep this colour going until the end of summer, grow 'Crimson Shower' as well.

All the roses in this group grow to 4.5–5.5 m (15–18 ft) and are ideally suited to arches, trellis and other frankly artificial supports. To bring more fragrance into the picture, add 'Débutante' in clear pink fading to blush, or 'Sander's White Rambler', which flowers rather late and has a rich fruity perfume.

Another group of rambler roses, no less generous but quite different in character, is typified by the famous 'Albéric Barbier', with its glossy leaves, much-branched growth and large, full flowers of creamy ivory opening from pointed primrose buds. It has the apple fragrance characteristic of this group of *wichuriana* ramblers, and though it flowers chiefly at midsummer, odd blooms keep opening right through the summer. At 6 m (20 ft) it needs ample space.

Even more vigour belongs to 'François Juranville', which has full flowers opening in coppery pink and coral, fading towards soft pink, and the same green apple scent. 'Léontine Gervais' and the longer-flowering 'Paul Transon' are similar, but their colouring has lasting coppery orange tones. In 'Auguste Gervais' the reverse of the petals is orange-pink, the inside pale apricot fading to cream, especially in hot weather. This and 'Alexandre Girault', which has full flowers blending copper, carmine and mauve-pink, are especially generous with their fruity apple scent.

'Emily Gray' adds soft warm yellow to the colour range; the flowers have just one row of petals, showing the golden stamens. The polished foliage of this mid-summer-flowering rose is mahogany-tinted when young. In 'May Queen' the apple fragrance emanates from blooms of rose pink flushed with lilac, borne with great abundance.

Roses with free-floating perfume

Whereas some climbers noted for their scents, such as honeysuckles and jasmine, are more potently fragrant at dusk and dawn, many roses seem to fill the air without stint all day. 'Rambling Rector' (also called 'Shakespeare's Musk' though apparently without justification) is especially generous, bearing quantities of creamy, semi-double flowers and growing to 7.5 m (25 ft). 'Bobbie James' is a little less vigorous, at 6 m (20 ft), and has good glossy foliage to set off its ivory blossoms. It is equally happy in sun or semi-shade. Another of similar size is *R. gentiliana*, which you may know as 'Polyantha Grandiflora'. In this the creamy white flowers have striking yellow stamens, and the orange-red hips that follow in the autumn are showy too.

Perhaps the most potent sources of fragrance among larger climbers are the wild musk roses and their near relatives. They are exuberant and generous roses, ideal for transforming a tall and boring Leyland's cypress hedge into a thing of beauty, at least during their early to midsummer season. In the wild they rampage over and through trees and hedgerows, so they will be quite at home doing the same in your garden.

The wild *Rosa multiflora* is endowed with a fruity, orange or banana fragrance often transmitted to its offspring. The flowers are ivory white and borne in large clusters, as is common with this group. Small vivid red hips follow in autumn. Its variety 'Grevillei' has been nicknamed the seven sisters rose because each cluster of flower shows many different colours, from carmine and purple to mauve and ivory. It is not quite so rampant as the white form, but still, at 5.5 m (18 ft) a generous rose. Another with lilac pink flowers instead of the usual cream or white of this group is 'Paul's Himalayan Musk', a strong rose reaching 9 m (30 ft), with small rosette flowers hanging in clusters on slender stems.

The Chinese *Rosa helenae* has fierce curved prickles, and can be used as a climber or left to make a huge sprawling shrub. The ivory flowers are borne in rounded clusters and are followed by vivid hips. One of the loveliest in this group is *R. longicuspis*, rather later to flower than most, with glossy foliage,

Opposite: *Grown on posts joined by ropes, roses such as 'Bantry Bay' make swags of blossom in summer.*

mahogany-crimson when young, and immense clusters of creamy flowers full of perfume, up to 150 in each bunch.

The vigour of *R. filipes* 'Kiftsgate' is well known, yet you still see it planted in quite small gardens. The original plant has filled three large trees, so you could expect it to engulf the average suburban garage or outhouse with ease. The white flowers, borne in clusters on thread-like stems, are very fragrant and open after midsummer. 'Brenda Colvin' is of similar character but has blush pink flowers fading to white. A completely new colour in climbing musk roses appeared with 'Treasure Trove', a seedling with coppery young growths and clusters of creamy apricot rosette flowers.

'The Garland' is an older hybrid, with very fragrant flowers composed of petals quilled like a daisy's, opening cream from coral buds and held upright, not nodding. The very tall 'Wedding Day' has a wonderful perfume of oranges, but the starry white flowers are spoiled by rain, developing pink blotches.

A rambling rose which has *R. multiflora* blood in its veins from both parents is the charming and very fragrant 'Goldfinch'. The little rosette flowers open from yellow buds but soon fade to ivory primrose, amid polished, light green leaves. 'Seagull' is very like a larger-flowered *R. multiflora*, a semi-double white with yolk-yellow stamens and a powerful fragrance. The clustered single flowers of 'Francis E. Lester' open from pink buds to blush and then white, filling the air with a rich orange and banana perfume. In growth this variety is more shrubby, ideal in a hedge or covering an old stump. Another bushy kind is 'Félicité et Perpétue', an almost evergreen and rather late-flowering rambler massed with double ivory rosettes opening from red-tinted buds. It is extremely hardy and tolerant of more shade than many, but is less generous with perfume than the musk roses.

Another that flowers at the end of the rambler season, after midsummer, is 'Kew Rambler'. In this vigorous rose single, bright pink flowers with a white eye are set off by greyish foliage, and give off plenty of fruity perfume. The fragrance of 'Splendens' is unusual in its distinct echoes of myrrh; the loose double, creamy white flowers with rich yellow stamens open from dark buds and are borne on branching growths.

CLEMATIS FOR EARLY SUMMER

Clematis and roses make a classic combination, whether on a wall or decorating arches, trellis and other man-made structures. However, you need to give a little thought to how you will prune your roses and clematis when deciding which varieties to pair off. The 'Albéric Barbier' type of rambler rose does not need yearly pruning, and thus combines well with clematis that flower on their old wood, early in the season. The cluster-flowered rambling roses that are better pruned after the blooms fade, the old stems cut out to make way for next year's flowering growths, go well with later-flowering clematis of the kind that you prune hard in winter. The clematis will peak after the roses are over, and you can defer the task of pruning the roses until the autumn when the clematis, in turn, has had its day.

Plants, like people, often refuse to fit neatly into categories, and several of the clematis that I am about to describe will flower early in the season if lightly pruned, or can be cut hard back in winter to flower from high summer to autumn. The criterion for inclusion here rather than in the next chapter is that, given the regime of light pruning, they will ordinarily produce their first blooms in early summer. As we shall see, double-flowered clematis have the quirk of producing single flowers on the young growths, later in the season. If you want to be sure of those full, frilled confections, you *must* go easy with the secateurs.

A few words on colour descriptions. Blue is a favourite clematis colour, with always a hint of lilac or mauve about it, so that blue clematis assort tenderly with pink or yellow roses and seem wholly in place beneath the grey-blue skies of cool-temperate climates. There is no clematis with flowers of the pure, almost turquoise blue you meet in some morning glories, a colour demanding the quality of light that produces skies of almost equal insistence. But since large-flowered clematis take in all the subtle gradations of colour from not-quite-pure-blue to a mauve that is almost pink, we have little choice but to say 'blue' for those with the least tinge of pink, reserving words such as lavender or lilac for the cooler half of the middle range, and mauve for the warmer. 'Red', describing clematis, is used to mean a colour with a good deal of blue in it, something more akin to magenta or, at best, crimson with a taint of purple.

Striped and red clematis

All the striped clematis of 'Nelly Moser' type can be lightly pruned to flower in early summer, often with a late summer or early autumn repeat. All tend to fade in hot sun; plant them in a lightly shaded spot. 'Nelly Moser' herself has mauve-pink flowers with a bright carmine bar on each sepal, while 'Marcel Moser', of similar colouring, has larger flowers but a weaker constitution. Another that can be a little tricky is 'Bees Jubilee'.

Of the two Barbaras, 'Barbara Dibley' has large flowers, but the rich petunia colouring fades disgracefully, whereas the bright purple with carmine bar of 'Barbara Jackman' contrives to fade pleasantly, so that you can grow this one in a sunny place if you wish. Another of bright colouring, deep violet with carmine bar and purple stamens, is 'Mrs N. Thompson'. Pinker tones belong to the narrow sepals of 'Lincoln Star' and lavender, carmine-barred 'Bracebridge Star', while 'Scartho Gem' is very free with its bright pink, deeper-barred blooms. The newer 'Carnaby' in raspberry pink grows to only 2 m (6 ft) or so compared with about 3 m (10 ft) for most of the varieties in this group; unfortunately it fades badly. 'Fireworks' looks promising, with catherine-wheel carmine and purple flowers.

There is more blue in 'Sealand Gem', the carmine bar soon fading from its rosy mauve sepals, while 'Souvenir du Capitaine Thuilleaux' is characterized by a very broad cherry bar almost concealing the lilac pink ground colouring. 'Doctor Ruppel' has rosy lilac sepals with carmine bar. There are, or have been, other striped clematis, but how many of this type can the average garden hold?

A few of the red clematis start to flower in early summer, including the

Roses and honeysuckle entwined together make a fragrant and colourful boundary or dividing hedge.

famous 'Ville de Lyon'. This, the first of the vivid reds to be introduced, needs good cultivation to produce a long succession of its carmine-red, cream-stamened blooms on 3 m (10 ft) growths. Taller 'Ernest Markham', in shocking magenta, will produce some early flowers if lightly pruned, as will 'Crimson King'. The petunia red early summer flowers of 'Jackmanii Rubra' are double, the later single.

Pink, mauve and lilac clematis

If these assertive colours are too much for you, there are mauve-pink clematis flowering in early summer, including the splendid full double 'Proteus', which has ample vigour, reaching 4 m (13 ft). 'Mrs Spencer Castle' is more problematic: sometimes she simply fails to produce any early, double blooms. Another double lilac-pink, less full than 'Proteus' and shorter, at 3 m (10 ft), is 'Miss Crawshay'. Among single-flowered clematis of this colouring, 'Kathleen Wheeler' has large rosy-mauve blooms with yellow stamens. 'Pink Champagne' has large lavender-pink flowers (nothing like the colour of pink champagne, actually) with a pale central bar and ivory stamens, on rather short growths, to

'The President' is one of the finest summer-flowering clematis, bearing a long succession of violet blooms here set off by gold and green Elaeagnus pungens *'Maculata'.*

2.5 m (8 ft). Even more compact, 'John Warren' has lilac-pink flowers fading to grey-mauve but enlivened with carmine margins and midribs, appearing over a long season.

Clematis with lavender or lilac flowers, by which I mean those a shade or two nearer to blue than those just described, make tender harmonies with pink roses, or gentle contrasts with soft yellow. Be careful if you intend to use them with the violet and mauve rambler roses; if the clematis is even one tone nearer to blue, it will make your 'blue' rose seem pinky-purple instead. A mauve-pink clematis might have the reverse effect, tipping the rose towards blue. Given the variability of these colours, the subtlety of their differing or matching shades, it is safer to pick sprays of your chosen roses and test them against several clematis before committing yourself to planting them together.

In early summer you can expect flowers from a handful of lavender and blue-mauve clematis. One of the first to open is 'Lady Londesborough', in palest lavender-mauve fading to silver, with crimson anthers. Deeper lavender-blue 'Mrs Bush' follows at midsummer. The flowers of 'Horn of Plenty', another 3 m (10 ft) clematis, open mauve-pink but soon fade towards blue. Similar colouring and vigour come from 'Lawsoniana', an old variety that still boasts the largest flowers of any clematis. 'Hybrida Sieboldiana' (what an inept name!) has lavender-blue flowers almost as large; another, more compact in growth, is 'Empress of India', its mauve flowers barred with deeper violet. The rich lavender flowers of 'Sir Garnet Wolseley' are enlivened with maroon stamens, and borne from early summer, as are those of silvery lavender 'Beauty of Richmond' and long-flowering 'W. E. Gladstone'.

The pale silvery mauve flowers of 'Belle of Woking' are full-petalled rosettes opening at midsummer on stems up to 2.5 m (8 ft). Another very opulent double clematis is 'Vyvyan Pennell', the lilac and lavender flowers full-centred with an outer guard of broad sepals, while the similar 'Walter Pennell' has the guard sepals marked with a carmine bar. 'Royalty' has double mauve-pink flowers. These three grow to about 3 m (10 ft).

The semi-double 'Daniel Deronda' has very large, deeper violet flowers over a long season (the later flowers, as usual, single) with each sepal bearing a paler bar. The foliage is bronzed when young, like that of 'The President', which is its single-flowered counterpart, in deep purple-blue with silvery reverse. Starting in earliest summer, or even late spring, 'The President' bears three crops of flower lasting into autumn, and still manages to grow to 3 m (10 ft). The shorter-growing Japanese 'Haku Ookan' has violet, white-eyed flowers, and 'Maureen' bears her ample violet-purple flowers on even more compact, bushy growth. 'Percy Picton' is at first purple but fades towards mauve, the large flowers borne on 2 m (6 ft) stems. Both 'Corona', in purple with crimson anthers, and 'Serenata', dusky purple with cream anthers, give you the choice of light or hard pruning to produce flowers in early or later summer.

Singing the blues

And so we arrive at the blues themselves, both the intense blue-violet of 'Lasurstern' and the porcelain blue of 'Mrs Cholmondeley'. 'Lasurstern' is one of the most popular of clematis, and no wonder, for its wide, richly coloured flowers with showy cream stamens are borne in early and late summer on 3 m (10 ft) growths. The more compact 'Lady Northcliffe' bears beautifully formed flowers of similar intense colouring all summer. In 'Beauty of Worcester', the early flowers are full doubles of rich blue-violet, the later well-formed singles with bold white centre. 'Elsa Späth' is a shade nearer purple, a single with self-coloured anthers; it grows to only 2 m (6 ft). 'Etoile de Paris' is as starry as its name suggests, with deep purple-blue flowers on similar short growths. Taller clematis of deep blue-purple colouring flowering in early summer include 'Lord Nevill' and 'Richard Pennell'.

The softer blues, matching Wedgwood porcelain or the flowers of periwinkles, are typified by 'Mrs Cholmondeley', her rather starry flowers freely borne on 4 m (13 ft) growths from earliest summer to autumn. At 3 m (10 ft), 'Mrs P. B. Truax' has soft blue flowers with ivory anthers, and 'General Sikorski' is characterized by the crimpled edges of its sepals. 'H. F. Young' is an elegant short-growing blue clematis, and 'Countess of Lovelace' another of similar vigour with full double, lavender-blue flowers early in the season, single blooms later. Both 'Mrs Hope' and 'William Kennett' are exuberant tall clematis that can be pruned for early or later flowers.

The worth of white

In garden terms, white is also a colour, sometimes a very assertive one, especially when found in large flowers such as those of a clematis. Bridging the gap between palest pink and white are 'Dawn' and 'Fair Rosamond'. The first has wide blooms with cherry pink anthers, the second blush white barred with pink around purple anthers. There are, too, some early-flowering white clematis with hints of ice blue: 'Edith', in glacier white with dark anthers, is at 3 m (10 ft) of much the same vigour as these pearly pinks. For very small spaces, there is 'Gillian Blades', its ruffled white sepals faintly margined with mauve, on growths of only 2 m (6 ft). Another with this icy colouring is 'Snow Queen', at least in early summer – the autumn flowers sometimes have a pink bar.

If you want a true white, declamatory and pure, you can give the famous 'Marie Boisselot' the minimal pruning regime to ensure early flowers. Her very large flowers have creamy stamens, while those of 'Henryi', more starry in shape, contrast white sepals with chocolate anthers and bronzed foliage. Both grow to about 4 m (13 ft), taller than the mauve-pinks of early summer. If this is too tall you could choose 'Mrs George Jackman', whose creamy white flowers with fawn stamens sometimes come semi-double in early summer. The old 'Duchess of Edinburgh' makes a speciality of her fully double white flowers, sometimes tinged with green, while 'Sylvia Denny' is a semi-double white with sulphur anthers. 'Jackmanii Alba' bears rather ragged, milky white flowers in late spring.

Both of the so-called large-flowered yellow clematis begin to flower at midsummer. 'Moonlight' is the shorter of the two at 2 m (6 ft), while 'Wada's Primrose' reaches 3.5 m (12 ft). A background of dark foliage in a lightly shaded position best sets off their fragile, pale primrose colouring.

COVER-UPS

Growing climbers successfully is often a matter of matching both the vigour and the character of your climbers to the chosen site. You can perfectly well grow large-flowered clematis informally, over shrubs, or in the conventional way, on a wall, as well as on pergolas and other man-made structures, while at least some of the rambling roses I have already described could be grown in trees or draped along a hedge.

As a rule, though, the larger, more vigorous ramblers that include the wild musk rose and its near relatives are a better choice for informal settings. They and other rampant climbers can be also used to do a cover-up job on sheds and fences. These relaxed ways of growing climbers can also be particularly appropriate for those plants that prefer their roots cool and shaded, as do most honeysuckles.

Many honeysuckles that flower in early and midsummer are generously endowed with free-floating perfume, especially after dusk. One of the first to open is *Lonicera caprifolium*, the perfoliate honeysuckle. The name comes from the way in which the upper two or three pairs of leaves are joined at the base so that they encircle the stem. The uppermost pair of leaves is cupped around a cluster of white to cream, delectably fragrant flowers. In the variety 'Pauciflora' the buds are suffused with pink. Both forms are vigorous twiners to 8 m (25 ft), very much at home festooning a hedge or in the branches of a tree, just as they would in the wild.

A cross between the perfoliate honeysuckle and the Mediterranean *Lonicera etrusca* is known, for some reason, as *L. × americana* (though plants by this name may be, correctly, *L. × italica*). This lusty climber, reaching 9 m (30 ft), has fragrant flowers that open white and age through ivory to yellow. Where the sun touches them, the petals are often flushed with red-purple. *L. etrusca* itself has bluish foliage, retained through mild winters, and fragrant cream to yellow, purple-tinged flowers in summer. 'Superba' is a selection with very large flower clusters, while 'Donald Waterer' has white flowers tinged red-purple, aging to soft yellow. They reach 4 m (13 ft), making them a good choice where there is not space for the rumbustious *L. × americana*.

The more or less evergreen *L. japonica* is even more of a thug, growing to 10 m (33 ft) or more, custom-made for concealing an eyesore, be it an ugly shed or a stretch of functional but unsightly chain-link fencing. The flowers, white aging to primrose and warm buff, are not large, but their perfume is far-reaching and powerfully sweet. The season of the Japanese honeysuckle extends from early to late summer, with a scattering of flowers well into autumn. 'Halliana' is a popular variety, perhaps the original wild form, while var. *repens* has flowers touched with purple. For cover-ups, the gold-netted 'Aureoreticulata' is less useful, for it has not the immense vigour of its green-leaved brethren, nor – unless it gets plenty of sun – does it flower much.

Some of the actinidias, to which the Chinese gooseberry or kiwi fruit (*Actinidia deliciosa*) belongs, are vigorous, leafy twiners that will cover a wall or a tall stump with equal enthusiasm. The smallish white, slightly fragrant flowers of *A. arguta* open at midsummer, and are followed by rather tasteless oblong greenish fruits. In its native Japan this climber reaches to the top of large trees. More familiar is the naturally variegated *A. kolomikta*, in which the leaves are tipped with pink and cream, the variegation sometimes almost entirely covering the leaf. It needs sun to develop its colouring, and has a curious attraction for cats, so it is wise to protect the stems with wire netting to stop them chewing a young plant to death.

In the family Vitaceae, to which the grape vines belong, there are some fine, lusty climbers too. I shall say more about the Virginia creeper, the Boston ivy, and others in a later chapter (see pages 90–2), for their chief glory is their brilliant autumn colour.

Opposite: *Climbers contribute to the densely planted cottage style of gardening, with every available wall decked in roses.*

You could lose quite a sizeable outhouse under *Fallopia baldschuanica* (syn. *Polygonum baldschuanicum*), the Russian or mile-a-minute vine which makes stems up to 12 m (40 ft) long. The leaves are heart-shaped, the tiny flowers pinkish; in the similar *F. aubertii* they are white. Both flower from summer to autumn.

The common hop, *Humulus lupulus*, grown to flavour bitter beer, is much too vigorous for the ordinary garden, but it has a golden-leaved variety, 'Aureus', which is a little less rampant and very striking, especially when contrasted with dark green or with purple foliage. In winter it dies down, so that you can cut the stems at ground level and yank them away from their host – be it a shrub, a hedge or a fence. In spring new shoots grow rapidly again to spread a cover of bright chartreuse gold foliage until winter's frosts.

The climbing *Hydrangea anomala petiolaris*, though sometimes slow to start, has ample vigour once established, and can reach 10 m (33 ft) or more. It will grow, though it may not flower abundantly, on a sunless wall, or can be encouraged to shin up a tree trunk like ivy, or simply allowed to sprawl into a wide bush. Like ivy, it attaches itself by stem roots; but unlike ivy, it loses its leaves in winter. The white lacecap flowers are borne at midsummer.

Fig. 6 *The cat's claw vine,* Macfadyena unguis-cati, *gets its name from the little hooks with which it climbs. Its trumpet flowers are rich yellow with orange striations in the throat.*

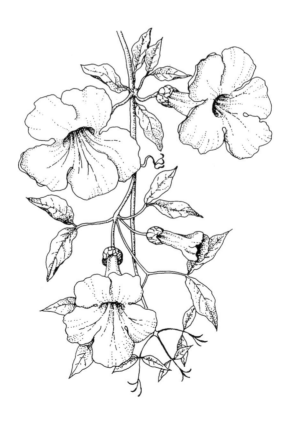

In warm climates the cross vine, *Bignonia capreolata*, is a good choice if you want to cover a wall or fill a tree. Evergreen except where the winters are cold, it climbs by leaf tendrils equipped with hooks or adhesive pads, and bears its tubular, orange-red flowers at midsummer. The cat's claw vine, *Macfadyena unguis-cati* (Fig. 6), bears yellow trumpet flowers in early summer, and climbs by tiny, fierce hooks on its tendrils. Both grow to 7.5–9 m (25–30 ft), and like most of their kin need abundant sun to flower freely. They are a success in high latitudes only when grown on a hot, sunny wall.

Most jasmines are too precious to waste in rough corners, on account of their poignant sweet fragrance. However, *Jasminum* × *stephanense* could well be used to cover a shed or outhouse, for it has ample vigour, growing to 7.5 m (25 ft) or more. Its flowers are pink, and it has an unfortunate tendency to develop white-mottled leaves that look unhealthy rather than properly variegated. The pink tone of the flowers derives from its parent *Jasminum beesianum*, which has deep crimson-red flowers, rather small and only slightly fragrant, opening in early summer. It is a vigorous climber with long-pointed dark green leaves, making dense growth up to 3.5 m (12 ft), or it can be left to grow as a tangled shrub.

WALL PLANTS FOR EARLY SUMMER
An evocation of sunshine

While scent, rather than colour, is the forte of the wild musk roses and honey-suckles, among the wall plants that flower in early summer, there is abundant colour, giving scope for some thrilling combinations.

By now the sun is higher in the sky, and the quality of light has changed so that the brighter colours no longer seem as garish as in spring, when freshness is all. Thus the strong yellow of fremontodendrons can be paired with deep blue ceanothus, enlivened with touches of stark white, or joined in hotter combinations with terracotta and scarlet. The Californian fremontodendrons flower over a long summer season, so you could choose *Ceanothus* 'Burkwoodii' which is no less generous with its rich blue blossom. When full-grown, *Fremontodendron* 'California Glory' (Fig. 7) will tower over the ceanothus, for it can reach 4 m (13 ft) on a wall. The matt green, fig-shaped leaves are backed with tawny hair and the same fur clads the stems; it can be a severe irritant, so wear gloves and if necessary a face mask when handling the plant. Better to stand back and enjoy the satiny, bowl-shaped, rich yellow flowers. In *F. mexicanum* the flowers are flatter and more starry, the petals deeper yellow touched with scarlet, on a more densely branched, leafy shrub. The cross between the two, 'Californian Glory', takes the best of each: the broader petals of the Californian allied to the richer colouring of the Mexican parent. Give them the hottest place you can find, in soil that is dry rather than moist.

The Californian tree poppy, *Dendromecon rigida*, grows with the fremonto-dendron in the wild and needs the same hot, dry conditions in the garden. Narrow, blue-green foliage is allied to satiny, fragrant clear yellow poppies borne in early summer. Not everyone's plant, for it can be capricious in captivity, it is beautiful when it succeeds.

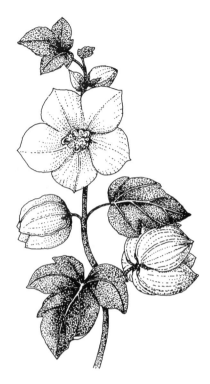

Fig. 7 Fremontodendron *'Californian Glory' is a showy shrub for a sunny wall, with vivid yellow saucer-flowers, ideal in combination with a rich blue ceanothus.*

Plants with pea flowers are a recurring theme, for this very varied and cosmopolitan family has much to offer among both ornamental and edible plants. The common names of *Clianthus puniceus*, lobster's claw or parrot's bill (Fig. 8), describe both the shape and the colour of its striking scarlet flowers, which hang in clusters from the lax branches in early summer. 'Red Cardinal' is a fine selection, 'Flamingo' is coral pink, and 'White Heron' is an improvement on the old *albus*.

Rather more tender than the clianthus is *Sutherlandia frutescens*, which also has leaves composed of many small leaflets, and bears its large, terracotta pea flowers at midsummer. They are followed by inflated seed pods; this is a plant easily and quickly raised from seed, making it worth experimenting with if you have a space on your warm, sunny wall.

The Moroccan *Cytisus battandieri*, despite its origins, is much tougher, and in many areas is grown as a free-standing shrub. However, with its silky, silvery foliage and pineapple scented yellow flowers in dense cones at midsummer, it is worth training on a wall. You could use its branches as support for a later-flowering climber that would look well against its silver grey leaves – perhaps a clematis like 'Etoile Violette' or, for a more startling contrast, *Eccremocarpus scaber*, the scarlet Chilean glory vine.

The tree mallow, Abutilon vitifolium, *makes a free-flowering wall shrub. This is the white form* 'Album'.

To bring a touch of sun to a shady wall, plant the spectacular but scentless *Lonicera tragophylla*, an aristocrat among honeysuckles with its long, clear butter-yellow, tubular flowers. Its offspring, *L. × tellmanniana*, is brighter, in coppery yellow touched with flame, but less refined.

The name of *Vestia foetida* is not very alluring: who would want to grow something that smells bad? In fact, only the leaves are foetid, and then only when you crush them. This is a quietly attractive small shrub for a warm place in mild areas, with abundant tubular, primrose yellow flowers from late spring to midsummer.

Soft colours on a sunny wall

Not all the wall shrubs that flower in early summer display these hot colours; you can also make soft-toned combinations of mauve, lilac and pink. The rose acacia, *Robinia hispida*, is rather brittle, so wall shelter helps to protect it from damage. It bears its deep rose pink, wisteria-like flowers in early summer. One of the most striking of buddleias flowers at midsummer: *Buddleja colvilei* grows into a big shrub or can even become tree-like. The large, rose-red, tubular flowers are held in drooping sprays; in the variety 'Kewensis' they are deep crimson-maroon. Though remarkably frost-resistant when established, *B. colvilei* is tender

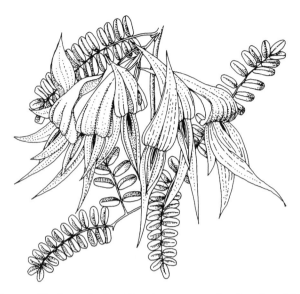

Fig. 8 *More of a scrambler than a climber,* Clianthus puniceus *has claw-shaped flowers in scarlet, pink or white, earning it the name lobster claw.*

when young, and is thus often grown as a wall shrub. It has enough substance after a few years to give support to a climber, such as the climbing snapdragon, *Asarina barclayana*, or *Rhodochiton atrosanguineum*, either of which would carry on the colour theme into late summer.

A scheme of lilac and violet could begin with one of the tree mallows from Chile, *Abutilon vitifolium* or the uncommon *A. ochsenii*. Large shrubs or even small trees, they will stand only moderate frost, and so do well against a wall. Amid grey-green, soft-textured leaves of vine-like outline, *A. vitifolium* bears wide cupped flowers of fragile, silken texture, typically pale ice-lilac, often white. They are easily raised from seed, but if you want to be sure of your colour, and of good-sized flowers, choose lilac 'Veronica Tennant' or 'Tennant's White'. *A. ochsenii*, which has deeper lavender-violet flowers, has been crossed with *A. vitifolium* to produce the very free-flowering *A. × suntense*. Again, there are white or lilac forms, such as 'Jermyns' with rich mauve flowers.

The flowering season of these mallows usually overlaps with that of *Solanum crispum* 'Glasnevin', the early-to-late-flowering climbing potato. Such a prosaic name does little justice to a plant that produces massed deep violet-blue flowers, each one enlivened with a bright yellow central pointel of stamens, over several months from early summer. It is a vigorous scrambler that, in mild areas, can be allowed to cover a shed or a fence, but lends itself well to wall-training to make a sheet of long-lasting colour.

The bead tree, *Melia azedarach*, from India and China makes a delightful street tree in Mediterranean climates, but is scarcely frost resistant. The extra heat stored by a wall facing the midday sun will help to ripen its growths to produce its open sprays of small, fragrant, mauve flowers in summer and the yellow fruits on bare winter branches which give it the name 'bead tree'. The foliage, composed of many small leaflets, is very elegant.

There may be places, under a window perhaps, where wall space is limited. Here a small shrub such as *Hebe hulkeana* may be the answer. Unlike the more familiar hebes with their long spikes of many tiny flowers, this bears large open sprays of lilac veronica flowers over neat, glossy green foliage. Others of the same style are 'Fairfieldiana' and the more compact, pinker-flowered 'Hagley Park'.

Rather more tender than these is the shrubby *Jovellana violacea*, which at midsummer has neat crinkled leaves and sprays of pale lilac helmets with darker freckles. The daisy bush, *Olearia frostii*, has large, semi-double flowerheads of clear lilac colouring set off by small grey leaves. Of all the olearias, one of the most beautiful and challenging is 'Henry Travers' (*O. semidentata*), a coastal plant that needs an equable climate with high atmospheric humidity to do well. Given wall shelter, however, to guard it from cold, drying winds, it may be persuaded to reward you with its wide daisy heads that open deep lilac in colour and fade with age, the central disc retaining its rich violet tones.

FRAGRANCE AROUND THE WINDOWS

One of the joys of summer is to be able to open the windows so that your climbers and wall plants can waft their perfume into the house. In this, the jasmines are unequalled, and the season opens in early summer (earlier still in frost-free climates) with *Jasminum polyanthum* (Fig. 9). The pink buds open into eloquently perfumed white flowers set off by the dark green, divided foliage.

Fig. 9 *The heady fragrance of the starry white flowers of* Jasminum polyanthum *carries far on the air. In cold climates it is often grown as a pot plant to be enjoyed indoors.*

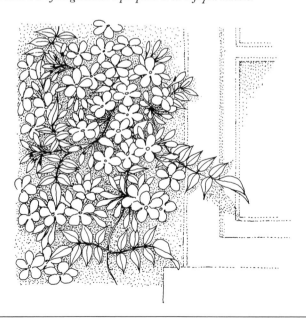

Olearia frostii, *with its large lilac daisies, is hardier than once thought, though it is safer in a warm, sheltered place.*

Give it full sun and shelter; it will stand a few degrees of frost, especially with the shelter of a wall.

The fragrance of *Pittosporum tobira* is reminiscent of orange blossom, and indeed the creamy flowers have the look of it too. This is a very easy-going shrub if sheltered from severe frost, tolerating drought and neglect and always comely with its glossy, blunt-ended foliage. There is a form with cream-margined leaves, 'Variegata', that is equally deserving of a place against a warm sunny wall.

You need patience for *Viburnum japonicum*, for it does not flower when young. The wait is worthwhile, for it is a handsome foliage plant with bold, highly polished, evergreen leaves borne on a shrub of about 2 m (6 ft). In due course you can expect rounded clusters of white, fragrant flowers at midsummer, and red fruits to follow. It is fairly frost-resistant, and makes a fine all-seasons wall shrub.

The unusual *Decumaria sinensis*, proposed as an evergreen wall covering in Chapter 1, bears its honey-fragrant, creamy bells in summer. Its deciduous counterpart, *D. barbara*, which needs more shelter, has white, scented flowers and can grow twice as tall, at 9 m (30 ft). Both are self-clinging.

Remember, too, that at midsummer your pyracanthas will be full of creamy, fluffy flower, in preparation for the brilliant fruits for which they are grown. But don't expect a delicious perfume: they smell, if anything, rather fishy, so may not make a perfect frame round a window or doorway.

CHAPTER 4

THE RIPENING YEAR
HIGH TO LATE SUMMER

IN HIGH SUMMER, some of the freshness has departed from the garden, and there's a sense of impending maturity that presages the poignancy of autumn without the shadow of winter's icy hand. Clematis and the repeat-flowering roses, more jasmines and honeysuckles, and the trumpet vines, are joined by annual climbers in a profusion of colour.

In a mixed border you can grow many climbers, especially annual or herbaceous kinds, through the branches of shrubs to give more colour in the same space. If this doesn't give enough scope, climbers on poles, or on a tripod of canes that you can remove at the season's end, add still more colour, and height too, in the least lateral space. Odd trails of the climber can be allowed to stray on to neighbouring plants, helping to give the border a unified, well-knit look.

ANNUALS AND THEIR RELATIONS:
WORKING TO KEEP COLOUR IN THE BORDERS

Sweet peas

The classic annual climber is the sweet pea, often grown in its own ghetto of poles and netting. If you want the flowers purely for picking, by all means grow them like this, but they can be enjoyed as garden plants too, especially some of the old-fashioned varieties. Names such as 'Matucana' and 'Quito' belong to sweet peas with velvety purple and maroon colouring and a swooning fragrance, while 'Painted Lady' is a delightful rose pink and white of great antiquity. Look out, too, for mixtures of old-fashioned sweet peas, which are usually offered in harmonious tones from pink to crimson to purple.

The perennial pea, *Lathyrus latifolius*, is typical of the scentless but free and easy cousins of the sweet pea that you can plant and leave to bob up again each year. The usual colour is a strong magenta pink, but it is also offered in pale pink, sometimes as 'Pink Pearl', and there is also the exquisite 'White Pearl'. The stems are strong and flexible enough for you to pull them about to cover a neighbouring border plant that flowered early and is better concealed at high summer.

The everlasting pea, *L. grandiflorus*, has spreading roots and large deep pink and crimson flowers over a long summer season. Both grow to about 2 m (6 ft). For something a little more restrained in growth, choose *L. tuberosus*, which has clear pink flowers.

In the Persian everlasting pea, *L. rotundifolius*, the flowers are of an unusual shade of coppery pink, among fresh green leaves. The most alluring of all the peas, however, is *L. nervosus*, which has fragrant, porcelain blue flowers, borne for months on end among greyish foliage, on 1.5 m (5 ft) stems.

Exotic twiners

In warm climates the kudzu vine, *Pueraria lobata*, can be a weed, but where the winters are colder you need to grow it as an annual, for its long spikes of fragrant, magenta-violet pea flowers on runner bean-like growth. The hyacinth bean, *Lablab purpureus*, is edible – in the Sudan it is a food crop – though grown in cooler climates for its ornamental purple or white flowers in summer. Start it under glass, and give it a warm corner, perhaps in a pot with some pea-sticks to climb up.

In cooler climates the morning glories are grown as cherished annuals, given a warm place in full sun to encourage their wide funnels of sky or turquoise or ultramarine blue, colours so much more precious than shades of mauve or purple. *Ipomoea tricolor* 'Heavenly Blue' is the well-known seed strain. The blue dawn flower, *I. learii*, has blue or violet flowers in clusters and can reach 12 m (40 ft) in frost-free gardens, scrambling over trees and hedgerows with the same vigour as the musk roses do in cooler areas. *I. nil* grows from seed to flowering size even in short summer areas, to bear its wide saucers of pink, lavender, violet, maroon and shades of sky and rich blue.

Climbing nasturtiums and snapdragons

The ordinary garden nasturtium, *Tropaeolum majus*, comes in climbing – or at least scrambling – strains as well as dumpy ones. However, the Canary creeper, *T. peregrinum*, is a true climber, an annual with bright yellow, fringed-lip flowers and greyish, ferny foliage on 4 m (13 ft) stems. The tubular flowers of *T. tuberosum* are red and yellow, among lobed green leaves; it is a lusty grower with tuberous roots and twining stems. In coldish areas you can lift the topmost tubers from each cluster to overwinter in a frost-free shed, covering those you leave in the ground with a mound of grit to prevent the soil freezing around them. The tubers increase so fast that you could even try eating them, as people do in their native South America.

Both these need sun, but *Tropaeolum speciosum* is happier in a shady place. It has frail-seeming, fresh green lobed leaves on slender stems, and bears in late summer vivid blood-scarlet blooms, earning it the name of flame flower. Try it through the stems of one of the white-flowered climbing hydrangeas, or on the sunless side of a dark conifer.

The soft pinks and purples of the climbing snapdragons (Fig. 10) belong in cool schemes with grey and silver foliage, mauve and lilac and pink flowers.

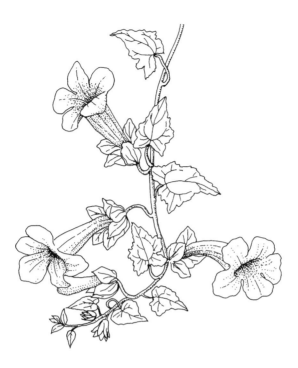

Fig. 10 *The asarinas are frost-tender climbers with flowers like an open-mouthed snapdragon – to which they are related. They can be easily raised each year from seed.*

They are perennials, but easily raised from seed to flower the same year as though they were annuals. *Asarina antirrhiniflora* has red-purple flowers like wide-mouthed snapdragons, on slender stems reaching 1–2 m (3–6 ft), while the fox-glove-like *A. barclayana* comes in mauve-pink, purple or white and grows rather taller, with velvety, heart-shaped leaves. *A. scandens* is similar but with lavender flowers. The creeping gloxinia, *A. erubescens*, has rather sticky foliage and large rose pink flowers.

Shades of red

Another frost-tender perennial twiner that flowers from seed in its first year is *Rhodochiton atrosanguineum* (Fig. 11), which has an unusual flower like a papery, muted magenta umbrella with a narrow, almost black trumpet hanging from it. The heart-shaped foliage is tinted with maroon. Try it with the frail *Ampelopsis brevipedunculata* 'Elegans', a modest vine with leaves splashed cream and pink. The rhodochiton also looks well with pale-flowered companions or among silvery foliage, perhaps that of *Convolvulus althaeoides*, a twiner with finely cut leaves and wide saucers of satiny pink. *C. elegantissimus* has even more dainty foliage; both will grow to about 1 m (3 ft) with support. *Calystegia hederacea* 'Flore Pleno' is a climbing bellbine with double, rose-pink flowers, needing rich soil and a warm climate.

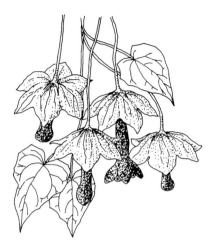

Fig. 11 *The flowers of* Rhodochiton atrosanguineum *look like a crowd of little magenta umbrellas, each one with its long hanging trumpet of deepest black-purple. Balloon-like seed pods follow.*

Opposite: *'Painted Lady' is one of the oldest sweet pea varieties still in cultivation. Its pink and white flowers are deliciously fragrant.*

Below: *The perennial peas lend themselves to draping over a host shrub, as here where their magenta blooms are set off by purple foliage. (Burford House, Tenbury Wells)*

Few can resist the tubby, cup-and-saucer bells of *Cobaea scandens*, a frost-tender perennial twiner that flowers in its first year from seed. Typically, the flowers open from greenish white buds, aging to deep purple, but in 'Alba' they remain alabaster white. If you appreciate the subtlety of white on white, try it with the annual Japanese hop, *Humulus japonicus* 'Variegatus', its leaves marbled with white. It comes true from seed.

One of the easiest climbers to grow from seed is the Chilean glory vine, *Eccremocarpus scaber*. Once you have grown it, you are likely to find seedlings popping up year after year. The flowers are little lopsided trumpets, most commonly orange, sometimes coppery crimson, with bronzed foliage (*coccineus*), amber with apple green leaves (*aurantiacus*) or salmon pink (*roseus*).

LARGE-FLOWERED CLEMATIS
IN THE FLOWER BORDER

I've always suggested there are many ways to grow clematis, but so often they are confined to walls, when they could be decorating poles or host shrubs to beautify a flower border. Following on from the varieties described in Chapter 3 come those that are hard-pruned in winter to bear their blooms from high summer to autumn. Many of those that flower earlier may go on to bear a second crop of flowers on the old wood in late summer or early autumn.

This habit is true of several of the striped clematis: try planting 'Scartho Gem' or 'Souvenir du Capitaine Thuilleaux' and prune them hard in winter. You can do this with the red 'Ville de Lyon' and 'Ernest Markham' too. There are several other red clematis for high summer: 'Niobe' has the darkest, velvety crimson-black blooms, very striking when set against a light background. The texture of 'Rouge Cardinal' also recalls velvet, though the colour is not so intense – a rich crimson with pale stamens – and 'Allanah' is bright wine red. By contrast 'Madame Edouard André' has matt-textured flowers of sombre claret with cream stamens. 'Voluceau' is petunia red, and the impossibly named 'Kardynal Wyszynski' has large crimson red flowers over a long season.

One of the finest mauve-pink clematis, 'Comtesse de Bouchaud', flowers from midsummer on. She reaches about 3 m (10 ft), taller than 'Hagley Hybrid', which has dusky pink, dark-eyed flowers over a three-month season. Some of the autumn-flowering varieties, like 'Madame Baron Veillard', need sun and warmth if they are to bloom. This is a vigorous clematis reaching 4 m (13 ft) with rather small flowers of warm rosy lavender. 'Margaret Hunt' is no less vigorous, and much less dependent on a sunny autumn to produce her neat, dusky mauve flowers. 'John Paul II' is even more willing to grow, reaching 4.5 m (15 ft) and bearing white flowers tinged with pink, sometimes showing a pink bar on the later blooms.

The name 'Twilight' suggests to me something bluer than its carmine-rose flowers, even though they do fade to soft lilac pink. A more truly lavender-blue flower for high summer is 'Belle Nantaise', with long pointed sepals. Both grow to about 2.5–3 m (8–10 ft). 'Lady Caroline Nevill' is another tall grower, to

4.5 m (15 ft), with lavender flowers; pruned very lightly, she may give you a few semi-double blooms in late spring.

In the deeper shades of violet and purple there are some fine clematis for late summer, strong enough in tone to hold their own against the intense colours of summer's flowers in Byzantine blends of purple, scarlet and even orange. The classic in this colour is 'Jackmanii Superba', an undemanding and strong violet-purple clematis that reaches 4.5 m (15 ft). Another of *C. × jackmanii* type is 'Star of India', a shade redder, with the purple blooms barred with deep plum-crimson.

'Gipsy Queen' is a lusty clematis reaching 4.5 m (15 ft) with rich purple blooms from late summer onwards. Another with great vigour, but needing a sunny, warm autumn to flower, is 'Lady Betty Balfour', her deep purple blooms enlivened by cream stamens. 'Madame Grangé' has red-purple flowers with incurved sepals revealing their greyish reverse. Paler than these is 'Victoria', in purple with a deeper bar but fading to mauve. You might think that 'Lilacina Floribunda' is pale lilac, but in fact the blooms are rich purple; like 'Victoria', it grows to 4 m (13 ft) or so.

There are far too few good blue, late-flowering clematis. You can prune 'Lasurstern' hard in winter so that it flowers later, and among the paler blues the same treatment would delay the flowers of 'Mrs Hope', 'Mrs Cholmondeley' and 'William Kennett'. But the true summer-flowering blues are 'Ascotiensis' in mid blue, and the incomparable 'Perle d'Azur' with Wedgwood blue, well-shaped flowers all summer on stems to 4 m (13 ft). Blue clematis look enchanting when threaded through the fiercely prickly stems of the climbing rose 'Mermaid', which bears a long succession of single, soft yellow flowers with golden stamens amid glossy foliage.

The two famous white clematis, 'Marie Boisselot' and 'Mrs George Jackman', can be both hard pruned for later summer flower. A much newer variety, which is in effect a white, more compact counterpart of 'Jackmanii Superba', is 'John Huxtable'.

Teaming clematis with pillar roses

Before describing some of the other clematis that flower in high and late summer, I want to consider roses, not least because hybrid roses and large-flowered clematis make good companions. Neither has much to offer in the way of foliage, but their blooms are so striking, and in colour and form complement each other so well, that other shortcomings are easily overlooked.

One attribute that is precious in roses and rare in clematis is fragrance, so my choice of pillar roses will be biased towards scented kinds. In this, few can rival the old thornless Bourbon rose 'Zéphirine Drouhin', its bright candy pink flowers continuously borne and distilling the very essence of rose. If you can't take that assertive shade of pink, try her pale pink sport 'Kathleen Harrop'. A taller Bourbon with the curious name of 'Blairii No 2' has exquisite, fragrant, two-tone flowers, shell pink around a deeper pink full-petalled centre.

Among newer roses, there is 'Pink Perpétue', which bears clusters of rich pink

Rhodochiton atrosanguineum is easily raised from seed each year to produce its abundant dusky red umbrellas each with its dark hanging trumpet.

flowers over many weeks, or 'Handel', its large cream flowers flushed and tipped with pink. Both are fragrant. For a pink rose with a touch of coral, there is 'Aloha', full of sweet fragrance, while 'Coral Dawn' moves still further away from the old-rose shade of pink.

'Phyllis Bide' is an old, fragrant rambler of rather short growth, bearing an almost unending succession of small, double, salmon and yellow flowers until autumn. Unusually for a newer rose, 'Meg' has scented, single flowers, but their colour, clear apricot-buff, is entirely modern.

If it's a yellow rose you want, to go with a periwinkle-blue clematis, but one of less vigour than the thorny 'Mermaid' suggested above, 'Golden Showers' is the one. It has double, clear lemon yellow, very fragrant flowers borne from summer well into autumn. 'White Cockade' is a charming, fragrant, long-flowering double white.

The viticella and texensis clematis

If you have ever mourned a large-flowered clematis that succumbed to wilt, take heart. A group of hybrids with the blood of *Clematis viticella*, though bearing smaller flowers, is resistant to this plague. *C. viticella* itself is a charmer with

Clematis and hydrangeas make a soft-toned summer combination, lasting in colour for many weeks.

long-stalked, nodding, violet-purple flowers in summer and autumn. It has a skimmed-milk pale counterpart in *C. campaniflora*. The hybrids with *viticella* blood range from white 'Alba Luxurians', which sometimes, seductively, has green-tipped sepals, to the sultry darkness of 'Royal Velours'. 'Huldine' has flowers of mother-of-pearl colouring, and there is a trio with white flowers margined and veined in mauve: 'Little Nell', 'Minuet' and, brightest of the three, 'Venosa Violacea' with red-purple margins.

The reds are often described as wine- or claret-coloured, but can range from bright crimson to a colour much bluer than any self-respecting claret. 'Abundance' is very free with its light crimson flowers; 'Kermesina' (syn. 'Rubra') has deeper burgundy flowers and is more vigorous, growing to 4.5 m (15 ft). 'Madame Julia Correvon' has elegantly poised claret-crimson flowers with twisted sepals on short growth, similar to that of 'Margot Koster' which bears starry red flowers.

The old 'Etoile Violette' has shapely blooms of rich violet with creamy stamens, while newer 'Polish Spirit' has large, deep purple flowers, and 'Elvan' has some of the poise of the wild species, its purple flowers nodding on long stalks. Another new variety is 'Betty Corning', with pale lilac bells recurved at the tips, and 'Pagoda' describes its shape in its name; the blooms are mauve-pink.

One of the most enchanting is the double 'Purpurea Plena Elegans', each little rosette a soft, dusky lilac purple with touches of grey, infinitely subtle. Despite its old-fashioned air it is a vigorous grower to 4.5 m (15 ft).

Those clematis with blood of *C. texensis* in them are a small group of climbers of restrained growth flowering from summer to autumn. Their colour range is unusual among clematis in encompassing pink, cherry red and crimson without that wicked taint of magenta. 'Etoile Rose' is of the starry outline that its name suggests, with paler margins to its cherry-crimson flowers; crimson 'Gravetye Beauty' also opens wide. Both 'Duchess of Albany' and 'Sir Trevor Lawrence' bear tulip-shaped flowers, the first candy pink, the second cherry red.

ADDING COLOUR WITH HONEYSUCKLES

Clematis and pillar roses are not the only permanent climbers that can be tethered to poles or tripods to add colour to borders of mixed plantings. Honeysuckles can take up a good deal of space, if you grow them in the natural way, through neighbouring shrubs or into trees. But you can tame their vigour by giving them a pole to climb, clipping them back to the support each winter. A honeysuckle on a pole in a border will probably thrive and flower with abandon, its roots shaded by neighbouring plants and its head in the sun. Some of the vigorous species already described (p. 50) could be grown in this way, with the early cream or perfoliate honeysuckle, *Lonicera caprifolium*, opening the season. Its flowers, though pale, are quite large, and look well in a border setting; and, of course, they add their eloquent perfume to any group they grace. If you want more colour, you could choose *L. × americana* (this, as we have seen, is the name by which *L. × italica* is frequently offered); in a sunny border, the buds are suffused with dusky pink, which lingers on the tube as the creamy flowers expand.

Lonicera periclymenum 'Serotina', the late Dutch honeysuckle, keeps the season alive with fragrance, for it blooms until the autumn. As with *L. × italica*, the tinge of pink on the flowers deepens in the sun to madder purple. 'Graham Thomas' is a newer variety with large, cream flowers, every bit as fragrant. The brightest of the scented honeysuckles is *Lonicera × heckrottii*, sometimes called 'Gold Flame', which aptly describes its yellow and orange-pink colour effect, the tube flushed with red-purple. It is bushier and, at 3 m (10 ft), shorter in growth than the late Dutch, and does best in light shade; however, it will grow well enough in sun if the roots are well shaded by neighbouring plants.

The very vivid *L. × brownii* 'Dropmore Scarlet' has no fragrance at all. Like the similar 'Fuchsioides', it makes bushy growth to about 3 m (10 ft). The startling colour is inherited from the trumpet honeysuckle, *L. sempervirens*, which grows to about 6 m (20 ft) and needs some shelter in cold gardens. The chief drawback with these brilliant honeysuckles, apart from their lack of scent, is that they are very susceptible to aphid attack, and because the flower buds are clasped between pairs of leaves, it can be hard to dislodge the pests; you may need to resort to a systemic insecticide.

Honeysuckles are invaluable for bringing extra colour to shady borders, where it is easy to create plantings with lush foliage and soft-coloured flowers, but not always so simple to spice the groups up with vivid tones. *Lonicera × tellmanniana* is a bushy climber with bright coppery-yellow flowers in large clusters, equally happy in shade or sun, and the scarlet honeysuckles just described all do well in light shade as well. Even quite deep shade suits *L. tragophylla*, a spectacular, though scentless, clear yellow honeysuckle with very long-tubed flowers, gleaming out of the shadows like a captive ray of sunshine. Perhaps the best of all settings for it is the sunless side of a grey stone wall, where it could join other shade-loving climbers and wall plants.

SUMMER FLOWERS ON SHADY WALLS

Not everyone has an expanse of baking hot wall to encourage sun-baskers to flower freely. But even if your only available wall space is shaded, there are still several handsome climbers to choose from as well as these vivid honeysuckles. By combining them with shrubs, you can furnish your shady wall with a planting of unusual quality, blending evergreen foliage of firm outline and light-reflecting texture with colourful or ethereally pale flowers.

Following on from the white froth of *Hydrangea petiolaris*, several climbing hydrangea relatives flower in high and late summer. The deciduous, self-clinging *Schizophragma hydrangeoides* is much more showy in flower, each cluster of tiny fertile florets set off by a large ivory-white bract, or pink in the variety 'Roseum'. *S. integrifolium* has even bolder bracts. Later, it is the turn of *Hydrangea serratifolia*, a self-clinging, evergreen climber with frothy, creamy blossom, and of *Pileostegia viburnoides*, which bears pyramid-shaped heads of tiny, ivory-cream flowers amid long, elegantly simple evergreen leaves. You could thread the flame flower, *Tropaeolum speciosum*, through these to add its touches of brilliant scarlet.

Fig. 12 *Until it flowers,* Desfontainea spinosa *looks very like a holly: but no holly ever bore these scarlet and yellow tubular flowers.*

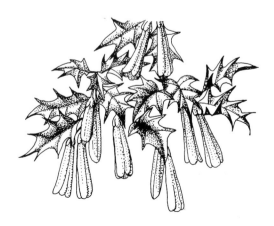

The pale, fragrant flowers of the climbing Bourbon rose 'Kathleen Harrop' stand out dramatically on this pergola against a summer-blue sky.

For more colour on your shady wall, you could turn to a shrub, a scrambler and a twining climber, all evergreen and all from South America. The shrub is *Desfontainea spinosa* (Fig. 12), which looks very like a holly until its tubular scarlet and yellow flowers open in late summer. Scarlet flowers like little plush-textured, bellied trumpets are borne by the scrambling *Mitraria coccinea*, and hanging clusters of blood-crimson bells by *Berberidopsis corallina*. All three prefer a leafy soil and shelter from cold winds.

The queen of climbers for a sheltered, shady place, without doubt, is *Lapageria rosea* (Fig. 13). The hanging, waxen flowers, narrowly flared bells, are soft crimson pink or, in the splendid variety 'Nash Court', pale pink with deeper flecks. There are also white forms of exquisite beauty, the flowers looking as though they had been carved from wax intended for the finest votive candles.

Opposite: *The small-flowered* Clematis *'Minuet' brings a light touch to these candy-pink roses.*

Fig. 13 *One of the most distinguished of climbers for a sheltered, part-shaded place is* Lapageria rosea, *its long, narrowly flared bells of rose or white looking as though carved from wax.*

ROSES ON WALLS

There are even roses that will grow on shady walls, though not in the darkest places: they need open sky above their heads. Despite her age, 'Madame Alfred Carrière' is ideal for such a position; her fully double, blush-white blooms gleam in the shadows amid the fresh green foliage. They have a delicious fragrance, and keep opening over a long and almost unbroken season. The grand old glory rose, 'Gloire de Dijon', also does well on a lightly shaded wall, though most other Noisette roses need warm, sheltered conditions and are described later in this section. The glory rose has a long season of richly scented, full flowers of buff and gold flushed with peach.

That pretty repeat-flowering rambler, 'New Dawn' – which looks, in bud at least, like a small-flowered hybrid tea, elegantly scrolled – does as well in light shade as in sun. The pink buds open to loosely double, shell pink, sweetly perfumed flowers set off by glossy foliage. Try combining it with *Lonicera × italica* to delight your senses all summer long. It is worth growing a honeysuckle with the old rose 'Paul's Scarlet Climber', too, for this has little scent. However, it still deserves garden space for its bright crimson-scarlet blooms, a little inelegant in shape but generously borne with a good repeat season.

The climbing sports of large-flowered roses are often grown on walls and, unlike bush roses, they tend to stay with us for many years. Most prefer an open, sunny position, though a few willingly perform on shady walls. Varieties from the early part of this century such as 'Shot Silk, Climbing' in salmon pink or the coral and apricot 'Madame Edouard Herriot, Climbing' are still grown. Among

Fig. 14 *Abutilons vary from those with saucer or cup-shaped flowers to* Abutilon megapotamicum *with its waisted, flared-skirt flowers of red and yellow, borne over a very long season.*

the cooler pinks 'Madame Caroline Testout, Climbing' is a full-flowered beauty with an autumn repeat, while 'Madame Grégoire Staechelin' (suitable for a sunless wall as well) gives her all in one great summer season of pale pink, fragrant blooms.

The old, deep velvety red 'Guinée' and 'Etoile de Hollande, Climbing' have all the rich fragrance one expects from a red rose, and a repeat season too. 'Etoile de Hollande' has the great merit of not turning purple with age. 'Souvenir de Claudius Denoyel', no less richly perfumed, has a touch more scarlet in its colouring, and does well in light shade.

The fragrant blooms of 'Paul's Lemon Pillar' have hardly been equalled for size, yet they are not coarse, and their lemon ice colouring is very subtle. This rose has only one flowering season. For a pure white with a repeat season, there is the old tea rose 'Mrs Herbert Stevens, Climbing', with scrolled, pointed buds opening to tea-scented blooms.

The usual Noisette colour is a soft or warm yellow, and most of these roses are perpetual-flowering, none more so than 'Alister Stella Gray', a charming and fragrant rose with flat-faced flowers borne in small sprays in summer and wide, many-bloomed heads in autumn. 'Céline Forestier' has paler, primrose yellow blooms touched with peach, over many weeks in summer and autumn. Its season is matched by one of the very first Noisettes to be raised, 'Desprez à Fleur Jaune', in creamy apricot flushed with yellow. The wonderful old 'Maréchal Niel' needs a very warm, preferably frost-free position; the nodding, elegant blooms are soft yellow and full of tea fragrance.

Small-flowered clematis such as 'Kermesina' can be just as colourful as the large-bloomed varieties, and have the advantage of greater disease resistance.

NEEDED: SUN OR SHELTER

It's fairly easy to define a climber: a plant that needs support for its lax stems, and often – though not invariably – helps itself to climb by devices such as aerial roots, twining stems or coiling tendrils. But a wall shrub is a much more elusive concept. Walls don't happen along in the wild for shrubs to grow against; planting against walls is the gardener's way of exploiting micro-climates to grow what might be too tender, or too brittle, or too little inclined to flower, without that extra help.

That is why, in these pages, I have included shrubs with very different hardiness ratings, which may have made you say to yourself 'Why on earth does she call *that* a wall shrub?'. Those I want to describe now, together with the climbers that accompany them, are all more or less frost-tender, or need the extra baking that the reflected warmth of a wall can give them in order to flower.

Opposite: Lonicera × tellmanniana *is as bright as any honeysuckle; it lacks only fragrance.*

Where space is limited

Extra-warm corners tend to be at a premium in most gardens, so I'll begin with some small-sized climbers and shrubs. *Sollya heterophylla*, the bluebell creeper, can be tucked into the smallest space, for it is a slender twiner with sky blue bells in summer and autumn; the very similar *S. parviflora* has smaller, richer blue flowers. They look well with the little, bright yellow pouches of *Calceolaria integrifolia*, a small evergreen shrub. *C. i.* 'Kentish Hero' is much the same but with deep rust-red pouches. The red and yellow theme is echoed by *Abutilon megapotamicum* (Fig. 14), a slender shrub with flowers formed of a deep red calyx and warm yellow, narrowly flared 'skirt' with a protruding club of stamens. 'Kentish Belle' and 'Patrick Synge' have larger, more widely flared flowers of softer colouring.

The shrubby monkey musks have narrow, dark green, sticky foliage and a long season of flowers ranging from the buff tones of *Mimulus longiflorus* and brighter apricot of *M. aurantiacus* to the deep, coppery crimson of *M. puniceus*. The apricot shades are matched by the sprays of clustered tubes borne by *Cestrum aurantiacum*. The whole range of these colours is displayed by *Mina lobata*, a frost-tender perennial twiner that can be grown from seed like a half-hardy annual. The narrow flowers, held in one-sided sprays, fade as they mature from rich red through orange and yellow to ivory.

One of the shrubby salvias is near enough to pure scarlet to join this group. *Salvia microphylla* var. *neurepia* has apple green foliage and bears its red flowers over a very long season. *S. microphylla* itself and *S. greggii* lean more towards crimson and magenta, though *S. greggii* has a delightful pale form called 'Peach'. The foliage has a slightly pungent smell reminiscent of blackcurrants.

The miniature pomegranate, *Punica granatum nana*, is a pet for small spaces, with its neat shining foliage and vivid scarlet flowers. Its bigger cousins need a good deal of space, but give you the choice of single or double flowers in vermilion or white. In hot climates the juicy, seed-packed fruits follow the single flowers, and you may even find self-sown seedlings.

Grevillea rosmarinifolia is an evergreen shrub that can reach 1.5 m (5 ft) in mild areas; it bears its showy, claw-like crimson flowers in summer amid deep green, needle-like leaves. If that is too tall, 'Canberra Gem' is only half as high, and bears abundant crimson-pink flowers. The pale yellow counterpart to these is *G. juniperina* var. *sulphurea*, with fresh green needles.

The charming *Tweedia caerulea* combines soft, grey foliage with thick-petalled, sky blue flowers aging to lilac-pink. It blends with other soft colours: the blush-white, satiny funnels and silver, silken-textured foliage of *Convolvulus cneorum*, a small shrub; the woolly grey-white leaves and short sprays of lilac-pink flowers of *Buddleja crispa*; and perhaps the fragrant, *Hoya*-like flowers of *Dregea sinensis*, white freckled with red at the centre. The dregea is a slender twiner which can reach 3 m (10 ft) in a warm sunny place.

Almost any fuchsia can be grown against a wall for shelter, but one that is especially suitable is the old 'Corallina'. Give it a wall at its back and it will almost turn itself into a climber, its long scandent stems set with dark leaves and scarlet-crimson and violet flowers from midsummer until the frosts of autumn.

Tender shrubs for larger walls

In mild climates *Plumbago auriculata*, half-shrubby, half a climber, can cover a good deal of space with its scrambling stems. Its sky blue flowers blend with any colour, but are especially fetching with strong magenta, a colour that needs a firm hand. At the start of its season it should coincide with the mid-summer-flowering *Abelia floribunda*, a shrub with long, fuchsia-like tubes of the most vivid magenta-crimson. The plumbago looks equally well with bougain-villea in all its colours, from the typical magenta to coral, pink and white.

The shrubby cestrums lend themselves to training against a wall to display their clusters of tubular flowers, varying from the scarlet of *Cestrum* 'Newellii' to the pink of *C. roseum* 'Ilnacullin'. In frost-free gardens they often flower from late winter onwards, but in cooler areas summer is their season.

A shrub with much more substance is *Acca sellowiana* (*Feijoa sellowiana*) which, where the summers are long and hot, should supply you with its green, fresh-tasting fruits. Even without these it is worth growing, for its thick-textured flowers, composed of crimson-pink and white, edible petals around a central brush of crimson stamens. The evergreen foliage is grey-green with a silvery coating on the underside.

The stamens are the showy part of the related Australian bottlebrushes, which come in a range of colours including the bright scarlet-crimson of *Callistemon citrinus* 'Splendens', in which the narrow leaves are lemon-scented. It grows to about 3 m (10 ft); if you want something rather smaller, try *C. linearis*, which also displays its crimson bottlebrushes in summer. Hardier, but less showy, *C. salignus* has long creamy-yellow or occasionally pink bottlebrushes.

Again, in the bird of paradise, *Caesalpinia gilliesii*, the stamens contribute to the overall effect, for this sun-loving shrub has long spires of yellow flowers with showy scarlet stamens, opening in high summer. The cassias belong to the same group within the varied pea family, and also have bright yellow flowers, though without the red stamens. In late summer *Cassia corymbosa* has clusters of bright yellow flowers, cupped not pea-shaped, and divided foliage, not quite so dainty as that of the bird of paradise. The much larger, bowl-shaped flowers of *Hypericum* 'Rowallane' are rich yellow and appear over a long summer to autumn season. It will grow to 2 m (6 ft), or reponds well to being cut hard back every spring.

In late summer and autumn *Escallonia bifida* bears its large sprays of white flowers, much visited by butterflies. It can build up into an imposing shrub with bold, polished evergreen leaves.

The appeal of *Itea ilicifolia* is quite different; among glossy, holly-like (but not sharply prickly) leaves, it bears in late summer long catkin-like tassels of fragrant, green-white flowers. In a garden I know it grows on a sheltered but rather shady wall with *Bupleurum fruticosum*, a shrubby umbellifer with sea green leaves and rounded heads of acid green flowers, and the variegated form of *Azara microphylla*.

The pink flowers of the late-flowering Clematis *'Duchess of Albany' have the outline and poise of a tulip.*

Decorating high walls with climbers

The cruel plant, *Araujia sericofera*, is so-called because its white or pink flowers, visited by moths at night, trap the unfortunate insects by the probosces, releasing them by day. The cruel plant is easily raised from seed and is quietly attractive with its pale, greyish foliage and faint sweet fragrance. More showy than this, *Mandevilla laxa* bears its large, pure white, scented flowers all summer amid bronze-green foliage. Its common name is Chilean jasmine, but it is related in fact to periwinkles and its flowers have the same propellor-like outline.

Another climber allied in name to the jasmine is the white climbing potato, *Solanum jasminoides* 'Album'. It has no fragrance at all and is even less hardy than its similar relation, *S. crispum* 'Glasnevin' (see page 56), but is so generous with its sprays of yellow-beaked flowers over many summer and autumn weeks that this failing can be forgiven. By contrast, *Trachelospermum jasminoides* earns its

Though it needs a warm, sheltered wall, Mandevilla laxa *stands some frost, and bears a long succession of pure white, propellor-shaped flowers.*

name by the fragrance as well as the form of its flowers, which open white and age to cream. *T. asiaticum* is smaller in both flower and leaf, making a dense wall covering in sun or light shade. Unusually, its variegated form is hardier (see Chapter 1).

One of the most beautiful of passion flowers is the white *Passiflora caerulea* 'Constance Elliott', which is fragrant. The typical form has blue-violet and white flowers. Their elaborate structure is said to have inspired the Spanish priests of South America to name them, for the parts of the flower, they imagined, represented the instrument of Christ's passion. *P.* × *caeruleo-racemosa* is similarly constructed, but its colour leans towards mauve-pink; it looks stunning among the purple leaves of *Vitis vinifera* 'Purpurea'.

There are many other passion flowers you could try if you have the space and a warm, sheltered wall. They range from the giant granadilla, *Passiflora quad-*

rangularis, which has very large, cupped, white or mauve flowers, the long wavy filaments banded with purple, to the long-tubed tacsonias such as pink *P. mollissima* or the vivid cherry red *P. antioquiensis*. If your climate is mild enough to succeed with these last two outside, you should also be able to grow the pink *Podrania ricasoliana* and *Pandorea jasminoides*, two bignonia relatives with the typical wide-mouthed trumpets of the family.

The scarlet trumpet flowers, *Campsis*, are very frost hardy, but need ample sun to flower freely. In areas where the summers are dull, they need all the help they can get from a wall facing right into the midday sun. The best of the group for such gardens is *C. × tagliabuana* 'Madame Galen', with salmon red flowers. Its parents are the scarlet-orange *C. grandiflora*, which climbs by twining stems, and the self-clinging *C. radicans*, which has a beautiful soft yellow form, 'Flava'. All have ash-like leaves which drop in autumn.

SITTING OUTSIDE:
CLIMBERS AND WALL SHRUBS FOR EVENING SCENT

The place where garden owners sit and relax – if they can tear themselves away from the weeding or mowing – is usually sheltered, sunny, intimate. It can be a place where house and garden merge into each other; furniture, plants – and even cooking facilities in the shape of a barbecue – side by side in the same paved or enclosed area, like a room with a wall or two missing.

The plants you grow on the walls that remain need to be at their best when you are most likely to be sitting out. That means, of course, that summer will be their main season. But more than that, office workers will use their sitting-out places mostly in the evenings, so at least some of the plants should have special after-dusk attributes. That suggests two things. First, plenty of pale colours, for they gleam out of the dusk where darker colours recede into invisibility. And second, evening fragrance. But scent in small spaces needs careful handling. Too many competing perfumes, and the nose is confused. One plant at a time wafting airborne fragrance is likely to be enough; you can, of course, add others which don't compete, those to which you must bend to inhale their sweetness.

The white, summer-flowering jasmines are endowed with a free-floating perfume that recreates in temperate gardens the perfume of tropical nights – not that jasmines wait until dusk to fill the air, they just become doubly eloquent as night falls. Where the winters are frosty, the common *Jasminum officinale* is the one to choose. Give it a sunny corner, and be prepared to restrain its exuberance. The variety *affine* has larger flowers touched with pink, and is even more vigorous; so much so that you could pair it with *Clematis montana* and let the two fight it out. 'Aureum' has both leaves and stems splashed with gold, and 'Argenteovariegatum' is more understated with its white-variegated foliage. For warmer – that is, virtually frost-free – gardens, there is *J. grandiflorum*, the glorious jasmine you find in southern Europe and the Middle East: the very name jasmine comes from the Arabic *yasmin*.

Also classically Mediterranean, myrtle – *Myrtus communis* – is an evergreen shrub flowering in high summer. It may get cut back by severe frost, but usually grows away again from the base. It can, in time (it's very long-lived), become quite bulky, so you might decide to cut it hard back yourself, in spring, once in a while. Both leaf and flower are fragrant. Brides in times past would always have a sprig of myrtle in their bouquet, and a cutting or two would be struck, to be planted in a warm corner as a memento of the wedding day. With the passing years the tiny plant would grow into a billowing 1.8 m (6 ft) bush, covered in late summer with its fuzz of creamy, many-stamened fragrant flowers, followed by purple to black berries. The variety *tarentina* has much smaller leaves on more compact growth, but flowers just as generously; 'Variegata' has cream-edged leaves.

The white-flowered form of *Buddleja fallowiana* can be grown against a wall, for shelter. Its foliage is white-felted, to gleam palely at dusk; the honey-scented flower spikes are composed of many tiny, ivory pips each with an orange eye. Its season is high summer to autumn.

Bridging the season between mid and high summer, *Carpentaria californica* is an evergreen shrub deserving a place on a sunny wall. The large, white flowers have bright yellow anthers and appear over several weeks. Golden anthers also enliven the single white, lemon-scented flowers of *Rosa bracteata*, the Macartney rose, which flowers on and on from midsummer. It is quite a modest plant, reaching perhaps 2 m (6 ft) on a warm wall.

A classic evening flower is the moonflower, *Calonyction aculeatum*, a twining climber that can be grown from seed to flower in one season. The huge white blooms open in the evening to release their heady fragrance, and close again before noon.

One of the noblest evergreens for training on a wall, given enough space, is *Magnolia grandiflora*. Handsome though the bold evergreen foliage, often backed with tawny felt, may be, the flowers are the thing. It is worth, then, buying a named variety known to bloom from an early age, as seedlings can take half a generation to reach flowering maturity. Both 'Exmouth' and 'Goliath' bear their great creamy, waxen, richly perfumed globes when still young. The first has long leaves with russet felting beneath, the second broader, highly polished leaves.

This magnolia is hardier than you might think, and in many areas where it is commonly planted on a wall it would in fact thrive in the open ground. The Asiatic *Magnolia delavayi*, which is more tender, is also far more striking, its foliage as bold as a rubber plant's, the surface of each leaf covered with a soft sea green bloom. The flowers are large, fragrant, creamy confections that open at night over a long season. Its only drawback is its ultimate size, calling for a large wall.

Although it is nothing much to look at, the lemon verbena, *Aloysia triphylla*, is an old favourite because of its fragrant foliage. Pick and rub a leaf and you will think you are handling the ripest, sun-warmed lemon straight from the tree. The shrub is tender and needs renewing from cuttings each year in cold areas.

CHAPTER 5

THE NIGHTS DRAW IN
AUTUMN

A S THE DAYS SHORTEN, the quality of light alters, dew lies more heavily on the grass, and a paradoxical new freshness inhabits the garden all the while the last flowers of summer are yielding to the fruits and the vivid leaf colours of fall.

THE LAST ECHOES OF SUMMER

The flowers that properly belong to summer, and that have a summery feel to them, often linger into autumn as though reluctant to depart. Repeat-flowering climbing roses may go on almost until winter, and the last of the large-flowered clematis, late-comers such as 'Madame Baron Veillard' and 'Lady Betty Balfour', are just beginning their season as their earlier sisters in the constellation of clematis are blooming their last.

You can manipulate the season of summer-flowering clematis to some extent, if you prune later than normal, so delaying the formation of the current year's growths on which flowers will be borne. But it is a risky game to play unless you can count on a long, open autumn. If not, your late-pruned clematis may not achieve its blooms at all, and your ploy will have been in vain.

If you prune the yellow lantern-flowered or 'orange peel' clematis hard back in late winter, their flowering will be delayed until late summer and autumn. This regime has another advantage; unpruned, they flower earlier but can quickly look untidy, full of tangled old stems, especially in winter.

The botanical names of these clematis is rather confusing, though many of us still think of them as *Clematis orientalis* and *C. tangutica*. No wonder we fall back on the nickname 'orange peel', which aptly describes the thick texture of the petals, though the colour is nearer to a ripe lemon's. The lantern-shaped flowers hang amid finely cut foliage and are followed by silky, wig-like seed heads. Both

Opposite: *Though it blooms in autumn,* Clematis flammula *has all the freshness of spring, even to the hawthorn fagrance of its starry flowers.*

flowers and seed heads make a striking combination with autumn fruits such as those of many shrub roses or the taller cotoneasters. If you opt to leave the clematis unpruned, it will quickly smother even a rose as large as *R. moyesii*; in this case, a fence or hedge would be a better choice of support, especially one that you would prefer to conceal. You could also pair one of the more vigorous clematis, such as 'Bill Mackenzie', with a Virginia creeper, preferably in a tree large enough to cope with two such rumbustious climbers; the effect of golden lanterns, silky wigs and scarlet foliage would be stunning in the autumn sun.

Clematis tangutica can grow to 4.5 m (15 ft) or more, so you need to be careful what you pair it with. It has a long season of flower; as a result, the 'wigs' that follow the first flowers mingle with the later blooms, silver and yellow amid the green foliage. 'Gravetye Variety' has deeper yellow bells, and 'Bill Mackenzie', already mentioned, is a striking variety with elegant, deep yellow lanterns followed by ample silky wigs.

The plant we used to call *Clematis orientalis* is now to be known as *C. tibetana*. The wild form known by its collectors' number, *C. tibetana vernayi* LS & E 13342, is striking with its very finely divided foliage and extra-thick lanterns. There is also a variety named 'Orange Peel', the name often used as a nickname for the whole group. Crosses between them include the rampant and rather coarse, small-flowered 'Burford Variety', 'Aureolin', and the uncommon 'Corry', very pretty with paler lemon flowers. The lemon-scented *C. serratifolia* has pale flowers with purple stamens, not long lasting but very plentiful in their short season.

Although utterly unlike the large-flowered clematis in both flower form and colour, the 'orange peel' types are both showy and exuberant. For something more restrained in looks, though not in growth, there is *Clematis rehderiana*, treasured for its profusion of small, primrose yellow, cowslip-scented bells in autumn. *C. connata* is even more appealing, with sprays of primrose bells on less rampant growth; it is likely to reach 6 m (20 ft), against *C. rehderiana*'s 7.5 m (25 ft) or more. If this is still too much, choose *C. aethusifolia*, a dainty creature growing to 1.5 m (5 ft), with very ferny, greyish foliage and pale yellow bells scented like jasmine.

Very different again, *Clematis flammula* is like a vastly superior traveller's joy, bearing a cloud of tiny white stars smelling rather like hawthorn, amid dark foliage. Its vivid whiteness sets off the scarlets and reds of autumn fruits, or draped over a wall it could form the backdrop to drifts of pink nerines, the magenta beads of *Callicarpa* fruits, and late Michaelmas daisies. It can be cut back hard in winter.

Talking of daisies in autumn, *Senecio scandens* is a scrambler, rather than a true climber, with massed clear yellow daisies in autumn and pale green leaves, bringing a sense of spring to the end of the year. Give it a dark-leaved shrub to embrace – a yew or holly, perhaps. In spring you can cut it back hard if you wish; in cold areas the frost will probably do the job for you. Yank out the dead or cut stems, just as you do with the clematis that you cut back hard each year, and the host shrub will spend the summer uncluttered by its companion.

AUTUMN FLOWERS FOR WARM PLACES
OR COOL CORNERS

In a warm, sunny corner, the red and yellow bodice-and-skirt flowers of *Abutilon megapotamicum* will still be flowering well into autumn, with the Chilean glory flower's lopsided trumpets and the dancing nasturtiums of *Tropaeolum tuberosum*. The sunniest places suit the trumpet creepers, *Campsis*, which should also sound their fanfare well into autumn.

Soft-wooded shrubs such as the coral tree, *Erythrina crista-galli*, and *Colquhounia coccinea*, enjoy the protection of a warm, sunny wall in cool climates. The first bears great sprays of rich coral-red pea flowers from late summer into the autumn. The colquhounia has soft apple-green foliage to set off its spikes of clear orange flowers.

In a sheltered place *Escallonia bifida* will still be flowering in autumn, and after a hot summer *Choisya ternata* will be indulging in a repeat season. Its autumn flowers are larger and correspondingly more striking than the tight clusters it bears in spring.

Shelter, rather than full sun, is what you need to succeed with the bell-flowered abutilons, sizeable wall shrubs with bold leaves – largest if you cut the stems hard back each year – and wide, hanging bells in a range of colours lasting well into autumn. 'Canary Bird' and 'Golden Fleece' both announce their colours in their names; 'Boule de Neige' is white and 'Louise de Marignac' a soft pink, while 'Ashford Red' is a fetching shade of crushed strawberry and 'Nabob' a rich, deep crimson-chocolate.

You need a cooler corner for the Scottish flame flower, *Tropaeolum speciosum*, which may still be flowering in autumn, and producing its blue seeds as well. The climbing *Aconitum volubile* (Fig. 15), also for a cooler spot, is quieter than

Fig. 15 *A climbing wolf's bane for the autumn border,* Aconitum volubile *has slaty blue, helmeted flowers. All wolf's banes are poisonous, so grow this out of reach of children.*

Above: *The lantern-flowered* Clematis *'Bill Mackenzie' bears a long succession of thick-petalled yellow blooms, mingling with its own silky seed heads.*

Right: *The scrambling* Senecio scandens *is another spring-fresh climber to bring colour to the autumn garden.*

these bright refugees from summer. Its hooded helmet flowers, a muted shade of slate lilac, call for understated companions that will not shout it down – it would grow well through the soft grey-green of a juniper or blue-toned conifer. You might like to try it with a pink escallonia such as *E.* 'Apple Blossom' – the two flowers would complement each other perfectly, but a coincidence of blossoming times is far from guaranteed.

MELLOW FRUITFULNESS

These late flowers are evidence of lingering summer, but the spirit of autumn lies in the bounty of fruits that the season brings. The queen of fruiting climbers is the grape vine. As well as those generous bunches destined for the table or the bottle, vines contribute to the beauty of the autumn garden. The bold leaves and dark bunches of sweet grapes borne by *Vitis* 'Brant' are a delight to the eye as well as the palate. Beware the black grapes of *V. vinifera* 'Purpurea', however; the purple that suffuses the leaves darkens the grapes before their time, so the eye is tricked into thinking them ripe, though they are too acrid to eat.

After a hot summer, *Ampelopsis brevipedunculata* should produce its clusters of small turquoise-blue fruits. Like *Vitis* 'Brant', it has plenty of vigour, reaching 6 m (20 ft). In a sheltered corner, even where space is limited, you could grow *Billardiera longiflora*, a slender twining climber with narrow, lime green bell flowers in summer followed by oblong, royal blue fruits. Though they look succulent, these are in fact dry capsules, in which the seeds rattle when you shake them.

Blue – true blue, that is, rather than black or purple bloomed with white – is rare among fruits. The Chilean shrub *Rhaphithamnus spinosus*, which needs a sheltered wall in frosty gardens, bears pale blue flowers that justify their existence by developing into bright blue berries. The shiny evergreen leaves mask sharp little spines, so this is not a shrub to plant where it might encroach on a path, especially as it could grow to 3 m (10 ft) in time if the climate is mild.

Firethorns and fishbones

The very name *Pyracantha* means firethorn, and many of these colourful shrubs are fiercely armed. But they are so generous in fruiting, and so easy to grow – especially now that varieties resistant to scab and fireblight have been developed – that they remain popular both as freestanding shrubs and for training on walls. They will grow equally cheerfully on sunny or sunless walls in any soil except a bog, submit to stringent training and clipping into formal shapes or can be left to develop as they will, and are undaunted by polluted air or cold, exposed places.

Varieties that are specifically said to be resistant to both scab and fireblight include 'Shawnee', which grows to 3.5 m (13 ft) or so and bears amber yellow fruits following its abundant creamy flowers; and the vermillion-red 'Mohave', more compact at 3 m (10 ft) or less. Others of similar dimensions are 'Golden Charmer', which has orange-yellow fruits, rich yellow 'Soleil d'Or', 'Orange Charmer' and the bright 'Orange Glow'; they are resistant to scab, while fire-blight is not usually a problem.

The older kinds such as red *Pyracantha atalantioides* and its yellow form 'Aurea' are said to be susceptible to both scab and fireblight. Several varieties, though troubled by scab, are said not to suffer from fireblight as a rule, even though they are not specifically resistant to it. Since scab can be controlled by spraying with benomyl in spring and again at midsummer, gardeners who do not object to using chemicals may not be bothered if their chosen varieties are not resistant to the disease.

Red-fruited varieties categorized in this way include the compact 'Watererii', tall, narrow-growing 'Red Column', 'Navaho', the vigorous *P. rogersiana*, and *P. coccinea* 'Lalandei', an old variety that is very free with its fruits. There are orange and yellow kinds that need spraying against scab too: 'Teton', a variety reaching 3 m (10 ft), and *P. rogersiana* 'Flava'. The tall *P. angustifolia* has orange-yellow, long-lasting fruits amid greyish foliage, creating a different colour harmony from the usual shiny, dark green foliage of the firethorns.

The related cotoneasters are sometimes trained on walls. For this purpose, one of the best is the fishbone cotoneaster, *C. horizontalis*, which sheds its leaves in autumn to reveal the gleaming red fruits. Paired with yellow winter jasmine, or with a Japanese quince – that will by autumn be set with its large, aromatic, yellow fruits – it makes a cheering picture as the days grow darker and colder.

Fruiting climbers, rampant or restrained

Unlike the fishbone cotoneaster, which can be tucked in beneath a window, some of autumn's fruiting climbers need ample space. The climbing bittersweet, *Celastrus orbiculatus*, is no plant for manicured corners, for it makes an undisciplined tangle of stems up to 6 m (20 ft) or more. Furthermore, unless you can obtain the hermaphrodite form, you need both male and female plants to ensure fruits, which are the whole purpose of growing a celastrus. The leaves turn to yellow in the fall, and the fruits are both colourful and long-lasting. Resembling small spindleberries, they split open to show the scarlet seeds in their gleaming yellow cases. Give it a large stump or an unimportant tree to cover; if you can see it with the sun at your back, so the fruits are lit by the slanting rays, so much the better.

The musk roses, as we have seen, can take up even more space than the climbing bittersweet. Some of them, having delighted the eye and nose with their clusters of flowers at midsummer, enchant once again when the small but abundant orange or red hips form in autumn. One of the best in fruit is *Rosa helenae*, with *R. longicuspis* not far behind. The wild *R. multiflora* has red fruits the size of a pea, while those of *R. gentiliana*, nearer to orange in colour, last long into winter.

The schisandras are climbers that are far less common in gardens. They need a moist, humusy soil and part shade; like the bittersweet, they come in separate male and female plants. The only one easily obtained is *Schisandra rubriflora*, which bears its red, fragrant flowers in early summer but is mostly valued for its 15 cm (6 in) strings of showy scarlet fruits in autumn. In time it will grow to 6 m (20 ft).

DYING IN SPLENDOUR

Depending on the weather and the appetite of the birds in your garden, ornamental fruit may last for anything from a few days to several weeks or even months. Bright autumn foliage, on the other hand, is ephemeral, and where the climate is inconsistent it may be a flop one year and a vivid success the next. But when it does die in splendour, the garden is so transformed that the gamble is worthwhile.

One group of climbers is unsurpassed for brilliant autumn tints: the vine family. It includes those rampant yet popular climbers, the Boston ivy and the Virginia creeper. Nothing can beat them for covering a large, bare wall or masking a stretch of fence such as the utilitarian, but ugly, chain link fencing.

Both in fruit and leaf, Vitis 'Brant' epitomizes the richness and abundance of autumn. Its grapes are sweet and succulent.

You can also grow them into a tree, so long as it is large enough to cope with their vigour, for they do need plenty of space, being well able to grow to 12 m (40 ft) or more both upwards and sideways. You can cut them hard back each year to restrain them, but it will be a task you can't afford to miss. If you can, arrange to site them so you see the autumn sun shining through the leaves, when you will achieve magical effects of colour and translucency.

The true Virginia creeper has five-fingered leaves; its botanical name is *Parthenocissus quinquefolia*, which actually means five-leaved. This distinguishes it from the Boston ivy, *P. tricuspidata* 'Veitchii', which – as its name suggests – has leaves with three lobes, rather like a thick, glossy maple leaf, but not actually formed of separate leaflets. Both are self-clinging and hardy. If your newly

At the half-way stage, with some leaves still green and silver and others turning crimson,
Parthenocissus henryana *is at its most elegant.*

planted Boston ivy refuses to cling, it may be that it has been too long in its pot with only a cane to support it, and as a result the suckers tipping the tendrils have dried up. Try cutting it back hard to encourage new, soft growth.

Either the Virginia creeper or the Boston ivy could be paired with one of the bigger, bolder variegated ivies, such as *Hedera colchica* 'Dentata Variegata' with cream-bordered leaves or 'Sulphur Heart' with primrose central markings. In winter, after the scarlet leaves have fallen, the ivy holds the stage.

If you have not space to do these justice, a better choice would be *Parthenocissus henryana*, a vine of great elegance, with fingered leaves often tinted with purple even in summer, the veins picked out in contrasting silvery white and pink. It is happy in part shade, and – unlike most plants with purple tones in the leaves – develops its best colouring out of the sun. In the autumn the leaves turn to crimson.

Among true vines, *Vitis* 'Brant' has already earned a mention for its fruit, but even if the summer has been too dull for the grapes to ripen, you should be able to rely on its striking autumn colours of mahogany, copper and orange, with the veins standing out in green fading to olive. The foliage of *V. vinifera* 'Purpurea', too, intensifies from its summer tones of dusky purple to rich crimson-purple. It is one of the finest ornamental climbers for a pergola or gazebo, where the sun can strike through the foliage to make patterns of light and shade rivalling stained glass.

The giant of the true vines is the glory vine, *Vitis coignetiae*, which can reach 12 m (40 ft) or more, and has immense leaves to match – rounded to heart-shaped and as big as dinner plates, so that it is striking all season. Its apotheosis is in the fall, when the leaves colour to a spectrum of colour from scarlet, orange and copper to purple-maroon, lasting long before dropping. Fling it into a tree, allow it to cover a shed or garage, or give it the formal setting of a pergola; wherever it may be, the adaptable *Vitis coignetiae* will enhance its surroundings.

And so, as with the first sharp frosts the fragile scarlet leaves of the Virginia creeper are dashed to the ground, the evergreen climbers that colour in winter – *Trachelospermum jasminoides* 'Variegatum', *Euonymus fortunei* 'Coloratus', and some of the many forms of ivy – begin to take on their cold-weather tones. The garden year has gone full cycle.

CHAPTER 6

CULTIVATION

WHETHER YOU ARE GROWING your climbers informally, in host trees and shrubs, semi-formally on a pergola, arch or pole, or carefully trained on a wall, you cannot expect them to reward you with a mass of flower or fruit if you plant them with no more thought than you would pull up a weed. You need to choose the aspect that is likely to be most suitable for them, and to choose the climbers best suited to your climate and soil.

Shady or sunny, warm or cool, sheltered or exposed, there is a climber or wall shrub for just about anywhere, no matter how unpromising. A little fore-knowledge will help you to avoid the kind of disappointment that follows when, forgetting its needs, you plant a sun-basker on a dark wall where it cannot muster the energy to flower, or choose a rampant monster for a small space so you have to spend hours hacking it back to keep control.

In the preceding chapters I have indicated the likely size and vigour of the climbers and wall shrubs described, and suggested where they are likely to perform best. It is time for some general guidance about soil preparation and planting, and the subsequent care of your plants.

SOIL PREPARATION

If you reflect that most climbers, in the wild, grow at woodland edges or among shrubs, you will need no reminding that they are likely to prefer their roots to be shaded from the heat of the sun, and growing in a cool, leafy soil. This applies even to many climbers that need the full heat of the sun on their topgrowth. However, it does not invariably imply a rich soil; in the wild, the host trees would be competing for nutrients with the climbers. Against that, highly bred garden climbers such as large-flowered roses or clematis are less able to cope with 'natural' conditions and will do better with generous feeding to produce the long succession and abundance of flowers we expect from them.

Some forms of humus also nourish the soil: well-rotted garden compost, leaf mould, bracken mould, farmyard or stable manure. Others, such as peat, ground bark, or coco fibre, add humus but little or no nutrients. Many gardeners are now trying to avoid using peat, which is a dwindling resource.

Garden compost, when well made, is the ideal humus to use at the time of

The climbing 'nasturtium' Tropaeolum tuberosum *flowers through summer and autumn before retiring underground for the winter.*

planting, providing nourishment and improving soil structure. As it does this with recycled ingredients – weeds, non-woody prunings and top-growth, organic household waste – it is thoroughly environment friendly too. You may hesitate to use it as a mulch, because the weed seeds it contains may remain viable if the heap did not become hot enough in the making; but well dug in it can do only good.

If you are planting your climbers in a border where you regularly feed and mulch, you may need to do more than excavate the appropriate hole, digging in a little more compost and perhaps a handful of slow-acting fertilizer, for each new plant. But when you are planting climbers or wall shrubs against a wall or fence, you may find that the soil is very dry and impoverished. Walls and fences keep much of the rain away, and at the foot of a wall you may also find rubble, old brickbats, lumps of cement and concrete – in short, almost anything except decent topsoil. This is an especial problem if you want to grow lime-haters such as camellias.

The extreme solution is to have the rubbish carted away and good quality topsoil put in its place. That is an expensive business, and if you are prepared to take time over the soil, digging in very generous quantities of humus and removing as much rubbish as you can, it may not be necessary. Much will also depend on how you treat your climbers and shrubs once they have been planted.

Opposite: Eribotrya japonica *is worth growing as a wall shrub for its bold, ribbed leaves even where the climate is too cool for it to bear fruit.*

PLANTING AND AFTERCARE

When you plant will depend on whether you have chosen bare-root or container-grown climbers, on your climate, and on the weather. Deciduous, hardy climbers, bare-rooted or not, can be planted during open weather – but not when the ground is frosted – during late autumn and winter in areas where the winters are not very cold. Where the winters are very severe everything has to be planted in one frenetic burst of activity in spring, when the soil has thawed but before summer's heat and drought add to your difficulties.

Even in mild-winter areas, less hardy deciduous climbers and all evergreens may be best planted in spring, though in very mild areas you could plant the hardier evergreens in early autumn, giving them time to make some root growth before their winter dormancy. This works better on light soils than on heavy, wet ones: a newly planted evergreen may succumb to winter waterlogging which it would have cheerfully withstood if it had had a full season to establish itself.

Summer planting of container-grown climbers and shrubs often gives good results provided you can ensure they do not go short of water, which may mean not only a good soaking for the roots before and after planting, and subsequent waterings as well, but also spraying with a fine mist to keep the foliage moist during hot dry spells. A temporary screen of shading material to help reduce transpiration may also be useful in hot or windy weather for all newly planted climbers.

Whenever you plant, soak the roots of your climbers thoroughly beforehand. Container-grown plants can be stood in a bucket of water to make sure the root ball is moist all through. Bare-root plants which have come by mail, carrier or rail, even if carefully wrapped, are likely to have dried out to some extent and should also be soaked on arrival. If you cannot plant immediately, wrap them in damp sacking and keep them cool but frost-free until you can.

How you plant is often just as important as when. A common failing is to make a hole too small for the plant's roots, and try to cram them in rather than extend the hole. The right way is to make a generous hole, digging in humus and, if your soil is heavy, perhaps some coarse grit as well. Lay the plant's roots out, making sure that they are spread so that they are ready to grow out and down, sift some of the prepared soil through and over them, firm it down boldly, and water in very thoroughly so that there are no air spaces around the roots. Make sure that you plant at the same depth as the climber was growing before. In light soils and dry climates you can leave a depression around the plant to hold water, but if your soil is very heavy and tends to lie wet in winter this is likely to do more harm than good. Planting clematis deep is recommended to guard against wilt (see page 106).

At the time of planting it is almost impossible to give too much water, unless the soil is already so wet that you shouldn't be planting at all. If the soil is at all dry, don't hesitate to pour a bucket of water into the hole before planting as well as another, or more than one, once the plant is in and the soil firmed over its roots.

If you intend your climbers to drape themselves over a hedge, or deck the branches of a tree, they will be competing for nourishment with an established host that will greedily absorb almost all the good humus you intend for the climbers. Once a climber is established, it should be able to fend for itself, so you need to devise ways of helping it through the first year or two.

One technique is to find a gap between the anchoring roots of the host, close to the trunk. The feeding roots of deep-rooting trees will be further out, so there will be less immediate competition. Against that, the soil close to the trunk is likely to remain dry as the leaf canopy keeps much of the rain away. Furthermore, some trees make a dense mat of feeding roots so that it is difficult or impossible to find a suitable gap. The alternative is to go beyond the reach of the feeding roots, and to contrive to lead the climber into the branches of the tree by a rope. Even then, the host tree's roots will quickly seek out a new source of rich nourishment.

It can be helpful to give the climber a head start by lining the planting hole with a bottomless box made of thin boards. Inside the box you plant in the ordinary way with compost-enriched soil. The boards will rot away over the next season or two, during which time your climber should become established without too much competition from the host.

After planting and thoroughly watering in, mulch your climbers and wall shrubs to keep the roots cool and to retain the moisture. Ground bark, leaf mould, coco fibre, even garden compost if you are confident it is weed-free, all make good mulches. You can also use stones to keep the roots cool, or gravel over polythene, but these will not improve the soil texture as humus-based mulches do.

Almost all climbers will benefit from an annual feed with a general purpose fertilizer, and a fresh mulch in spring, on moist soil. During dry spells, especially in spring and summer, you may need to give additional water. Don't stint; you need to give the equivalent of about 2.5 cm (1 in) of rain every week to ten days. Good deep soakings at intervals do more good than sprinkling the surface every day; indeed, this is actually harmful, encouraging the roots to come to the surface for the moisture, which leaves them far more vulnerable to subsequent dry spells than before.

WINTER PROTECTION

Climbers and wall shrubs may need protection against damage by frost and cold, cutting winds. Young plants may be susceptible to temperatures that more mature ones, having formed some wood, can withstand easily; *Buddleja colvilei* is one such example. Others may be on the borderline of hardiness in your climate, and need protecting every winter in case an exceptionally severe spell of weather should prove too much for them.

In some cases it is enough to make sure that the roots do not freeze. Climbers such as the hardier passion flowers (*Passiflora* spp.) or the Chilean glory flower (*Eccremocarpus scaber*) are capable of growing away again from below ground, even if the top growth is killed by frost, so long as the soil does not freeze around

Vitis coignetiae *has the largest leaves of any hardy vine, great dinner plates that colour to rich shades of crimson and purple in autumn.*

their roots. A generous mulch of grit, ground bark, straw or bracken should take care of this, at least through a normal winter, in areas where prolonged severe frosts are rare.

Others, together with the less hardy wall shrubs, may need fuller protection so that their woody framework remains undamaged. Evergreens, especially while still small, can be protected by bracken, conifer branches, a wrap of proprietary windscreening or horticultural fleece, or screens made of two layers of wire netting with straw or bracken between, which may be enough to shelter them from cutting winds. This should help to save them from cold-induced desiccation rather than actual freezing.

If you need to go further than this, and especially if you need to protect the plants against damp as well as cold, you may need to construct a plastic jacket for them. Except in very cold spells, the plastic should not enclose the plant completely, because of the risk of moulds forming in the damp, still atmosphere within the cover. It is better to make a frame around the plant to keep the plastic from touching it; in very cold spells, the space between the jacket and the climber or shrub can be stuffed with bracken or straw to insulate it.

PRUNING

There are several reasons for pruning: to remove diseased, damaged or dead growths; to ensure the maximum display of flower or fruit; to keep plants within bounds; to help them build up a well-shaped woody framework. If you bear in mind, when approaching your climber or shrub with secateurs, what you intend to achieve, you are likely to find that the task becomes less daunting. Mostly, it is a matter of common sense.

Always use sharp tools; this will help you to make clean cuts that leave no snags or torn stems. Apart from being ugly, snagged cuts invite disease spores

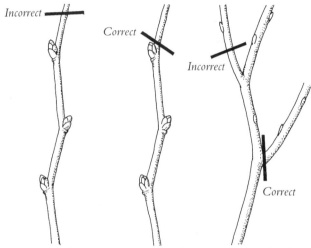

Fig. 16 *Whenever you make a pruning cut, be sure that your secateurs or knife are really sharp, so that the cut is clean and you leave no snags. Cut immediately above a suitable bud. If you are removing a sideshoot completely, cut it back flush with the main stem. If you leave snags or stumps they will die back, and the dead wood is a potential source of infection for disease.*

because they take longer to heal. Dirty tools, too, can spread disease. Make your cuts just above a bud, slanting the cut slightly downwards from the side on which the bud is forming (Fig. 16).

What to prune

What to remove? Dead and diseased stems, first of all, back to sound wood. Thin, spindly growths are also usually better removed. If the climber or shrub you are addressing is mature, there may be some old, outworn stems that should also be taken out to encourage strong young growths (Fig. 17); try to take these superannuated stems out as near to ground level as possible. Some climbers regularly produce strong new stems from or near the base, while others make new growths from part way up an old stem, suggesting a cut just above the young shoot.

If you are pruning to encourage a shapely framework of branches, you will need to consider with each cut the likely future effect. Does the bud you propose

Fig. 17 *Some climbers are best pruned by the removal of the oldest stems, back to a strong young shoot as near to the base of the plant as possible. This method is suitable for actinidias,* Campsis, Hydrangea petiolaris, *many vines, and clematis that flower in the spring. If you can disentangle their twining stems, it also works well with honeysuckles. Large-flowered climbing roses can also be kept clothed with strong young wood with this method.*

to encourage, by cutting just above it, point in the direction you want the plant to grow? If not, can you identify a more suitable potential growth? A rule of thumb would be to cut to outward-facing buds; but there may be times when you want new growth to furnish the centre of the plant rather than spread still further outwards. Crossing growths are best dealt with so that only one remains.

When to prune

When and how often to prune are questions that exercise the beginner gardener as much as how to prune. The first opportunity you have to practise the art is on a newly planted climber or shrub. I have to say that there are at least two schools of thought on this. One says prune lightly until the framework of branches has grown to fill the space available. The other says prune quite hard in the first spring after planting, to encourage strong, low-branching growth. The compromise is to remove all spindly stems, or cut them back to the plumpest bud available, in the hope of stimulating stronger growths, but to leave well alone if the plant already shows signs of forming good strong wood. If there is nothing but weak growths and a poor root system, you have been had, and should claim your money back.

The next decision you face is what time of year should you prune, and do you have to do it every year? Some climbers can be left alone for years; the opportunities for pruning a clematis, wild musk rose or honeysuckle growing in a host tree are limited, and you may decide to let things go as they would in nature. The result is likely to be, in time, a tangle of stems, and smaller – though not necessarily fewer – flowers. Even on a wall, you can let a *Clematis montana*, say, have its head year after year, and accept the bird's nest clutter of old stems as part of the price. Sooner or later you may feel the price is too high, or the climber may simply have become far too large for its space, so you cut the plant back ruthlessly, which may or may not kill it.

If this seems the possible outcome of inaction, and it bothers you in advance, it is better to decide from the outset to prune each year. Provided the mismatch between the climber's vigour and the available space is not too great, the result will be to give you larger, but probably fewer, flowers on growth that remains comely and restrained.

The time of year to prune is easier to decide. If the climber flowers on the current year's growths, which is generally the case with those that flower from midsummer on, you prune in late winter or early spring, so that the new growths have a long growing period in which to form the year's crop of flowers and fruits. If, on the other hand, a climber flowers early in the year, it will do so on last year's growths. Evidently, you must not prune these in winter because you will be cutting away the blooms to come. Prune them immediately after flowering, or even while in flower, when you can use the cut stems for the house.

Clematis

I have already suggested, when describing clematis, that different pruning regimes give different results. The large-flowered clematis seem to present the greatest difficulty, but here too the rule of thumb applies. Those that flower on last year's growths are lightly pruned, with dead stems cut right out and healthy ones merely cut back to the topmost bud, in late winter. The ones that flower on new growths, that is all those that flower after midsummer, often going on into autumn, are pruned hard back in late winter. Several will flower on either the old or the new growths, according to the treatment you give them. Good catalogues tell you which are which.

Roses

Roses need different treatment according to their type. Most rambler roses flower only once, around midsummer. After the blooms fade the flowered stems are cut out, as near to the ground as possible, and new strong stems trained in their place to bear next summer's blooms.

The ramblers that give a second crop of flowers are less generous with replacement stems. The best way to treat these is to remove some of the older wood

Unusually, this yellow-berried pyracantha has been paired with the waxy-belled Lapageria rosea.

each year. The wild musk roses and the vigorous *wichuraiana* ramblers, which are generally grown informally on hedgerows or in trees, are seldom pruned, though it is helpful from time to time, if you can, to remove weak and twiggy stems.

Large-flowered climbing roses often bear a second flush of bloom. They are pruned in late winter, when you should remove weak, twiggy growths and shorten flowering side shoots back to two to four buds. Keep an eye out for strong new shoots forming at the base, and nurture them, for in time you should be able to cut out very old stems and encourage the new ones to develop in their place.

Wisteria

Wisterias are sometimes the despair of their owners because they make masses of leafy growth, but hardly flower. The remedy may lie in correct pruning (Fig. 18). In the early years it is normal for wisterias to make growth, not flowers, but even at this stage you can prune to encourage the growths that will bear flowers in the future. Tie in the shoots to the structure they are to cover, thinning them out to encourage stouter and stronger growths. Twice a year, prune the laterals

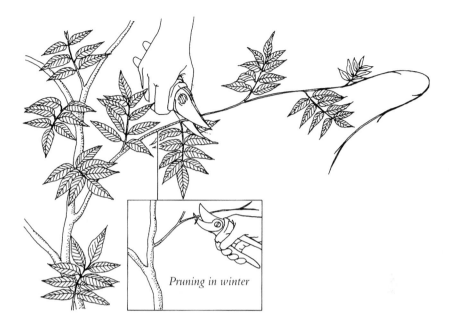

Pruning in winter

Fig. 18 *A wisteria that refuses to flower may not be getting the right pruning treatment. In summer, train long leading stems in the direction you want the plant to grow, and cut back any unwanted growths to 15–30cm (6–12in) from their base. This helps to encourage the formation of flowering spurs. In winter, shorten the shoots still further back, to two or three buds from their base. If you want to avoid winter pruning, pinch the wisteria back every two weeks during summer, taking each shoot back to about 10cm (4in), and later doing the same to any extension growths.*

(side shoots) of the growths you are retaining. In summer the laterals are shortened to about 15 cm (6 in), and in winter you cut them right back to two or three buds.

Keep this up for the life of the wisteria, and you will be encouraging flowering spurs that should fulfil your hopes of curtains of fragrant, lilac or white flowers in early summer, year after year.

METHODS OF SUPPORT

Climbers attach themselves in a variety of ways. Some are self-sticking, clinging to a wall, tree trunk or fence by means of aerial roots like ivy, or adhesive tendrils like Virginia creeper. Most need to twine around or hook themselves on to some kind of support. Honeysuckle and wisteria are two familiar examples of climbers that reach upwards by twining their stems around the branches of their host. Others, such as clematis, coil their leaf stalks around smaller twigs and branches, while sweet peas have coiling tendrils derived from leaves, and the cat's claw vine (*Macfadyena unguis-cati*) has hooked tendrils. Roses are regarded as scramblers rather than true climbers; their scandent stems grow through the host's supporting branches and are kept in place by their hooked prickles. Even less tenacious than this are plants such as *Senecio scandens*, which have long, lax stems weaving their way through neighbouring shrubs, without any means of attachment.

Once you know how your chosen climber would behave in the wild, it is easier to decide what support to give it in the garden. Only self-stickers can be left to cover a wall or fence without assistance, though they too may benefit from discreet help in the early stages, even if it is only a cane holding the stems against the wall until they have found a purchase. Climbers that twine or coil will need wires or netting or trellis attached to wherever you propose to grow them, to simulate the branches and twigs of a host plant.

If you are wiring up a wall, the bolts known as vine eyes are ideal (Fig. 19), long enough to leave up to 10 cm (4 in) space so that some of the climber's stems can find their way behind the wires. You can simply string the wires horizontally, or include vertical wires as well to make a wide mesh over the surface. Use braided wire rather than plain galvanized, which sags with time, and include tensioning bolts to make sure the wire is stretched tight. Instead of vine eyes you can use specially shaped nails with a hole for the wire in the broad end, but it is much harder both to fix them firmly in the wall and to get the wires taut.

If you use trellis on the wall, be sure that here too you leave a space of 10 cm (4 in) or so between trellis and wall (Fig. 20). There are many different kinds of

Fig. 19 *Vine eyes are ideal for fixing wires to a wall – drill the wall, plug it and screw in the vine eyes. If you use straining bolts as well, and choose braided wire, not plain, you can ensure that the wire is tautly strained and will not sag. Choose long vine eyes so that you can leave a good space between the wires and the wall.*

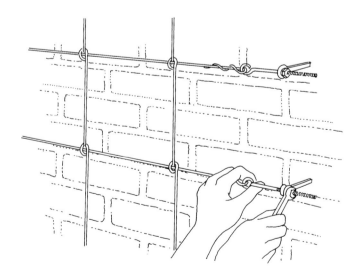

trellis, from elaborate purpose-made wooden structures to ready-made plastic covered mesh. It may be possible to fix your trellis so that when the house needs repainting you can detach the panels and lay them on supports without having to untie or cut back your climbers, though this only works with plants that have flexible stems.

Some fences, such as chain link or chestnut paling, are ideal supports for climbers. Post and rail fences are almost as good, though you may need to give the climbers some discreet help by tying in the stems with soft green garden twine or a plant tie fixed to a discreet staple. Solid fences of the larch-lap variety are more like a wall, so far as a climber is concerned, and may need wiring – stretch the wires between the uprights, using vine eyes for preference just as on a wall. A little help may be needed, too, for climbers on poles or the uprights of pergolas. The more vigorous climbers that you choose for the cross members of a pergola, or for an arch, should take care of themselves once they have grown tall enough to reach the horizontals.

Climbers in shrubs should be able to look after themselves, but those that you want to encourage into the branches of a tree are likely to need help at first. A cane or a stout rope will provide support until the climber has involved itself properly with the branches of the host tree. Remember that planting to windward is safer, because the prevailing winds tend to blow the climber more firmly

Fig. 20 *Trellis can look decorative on a wall, and if you grow supple climbers on it and need to remove them for re-pointing or rendering the wall at any time, you should be able simply to unbolt the whole thing and gently lay it on the ground while the work is being done. When fixing it, leave a space between the trellis and the wall to allow air to circulate among the climber's stems.*

into the tree. Be prepared, if a freak gale from the wrong direction wrests some stems away from the host branches, to guide them back into place with a long forked stick. Twiners are less likely to be a problem than scramblers such as roses, which rely on their hooked prickles to reach upwards.

DISEASES

Apart from highly bred climbers such as hybrid rambler roses or large-flowered clematis, most are gratifyingly free of diseases. Some rambler roses tend to suffer from powdery mildew, which is worst in dry, still conditions; never grow them on a wall, but always where they can benefit from the breeze blowing through their stems. It shows as a white, powdery film on the leaves, buds and stems and is more disfiguring than damaging, but can be controlled by fungicides. Climbing roses may also suffer, just as their bush varieties may, from black spot or rust. Hygiene is very important: remove all fallen leaves at the year's end and burn them – never compost them. If you see the characteristic black spots or rusty freckles which give the two diseases their names, spray with a proprietary fungicide and pick off affected leaves. Very badly rust-infected roses may not recover, and should be removed and burnt.

The fungal problem that can plague large-flowered clematis is known as wilt. It is a kind of sudden death, either of one or more stems or, sometimes, of the entire top growth. Cut out the affected stems, and spray the rest, and the soil at the base of the plant, with fungicide at regular intervals. Even if you have had to remove the entire top growth, provided you planted your clematis deeply, there should be a pair of buds below ground in reserve which can grow again. Watch for slugs, which can all too easily demolish the tentative new shoots as they emerge. Species clematis and their near relations, including the viticella hybrids, are seldom if ever affected.

Botrytis, also known as grey mould, plagues plants grown under glass in damp, chilly conditions, and can be a problem in wet seasons. Pick off all parts of the plant on which the grey, furry coating forms, as well as any dead leaves: the fungus settles first on dead material, from which it invades living tissues.

Rarely, you may find a honeysuckle affected by silverleaf, a common disease of plums. Cut out all infected stems back to healthy wood, and burn them.

In older gardens especially, honey fungus can be a problem, affecting all kinds of woody plants including climbers. If a treasured climber is attacked, you could try treating it with one of the proprietary fungicides that some people find effective, others not. Good cultivation helps; a healthy plant is less likely to succumb to an infection than a weak or stressed one. That, indeed, is true of all diseases.

Plants with distorted or discoloured leaves or shoots, and which seem stunted, may be suffering from virus disease, spread by aphids. Infected plants should be removed and burnt. The more you control aphids, the less likely you are to suffer

Opposite: *In frost-free areas, or in a conservatory, the bougainvilleas are valued for the long-lasting, vivid colour of their papery bracts.*

the spread of virus diseases, though admittedly there is not much you can do about your neighbours' aphids.

PESTS

Greenfly and blackfly, collectively known as aphids, are a common and annoying pest of a wide range of plants. They are sap-sucking insects, and their attentions result in stunted or deformed growths and fewer flowers than normal. They also exude honeydew on the leaves, on which black sooty moulds may grow. Honeysuckles are especially susceptible to aphid damage; the insects lurk inside the clasping leaves and are almost impossible to dislodge using contact spray insecticides. A systemic pesticide is the answer here. On many plants minor infestations can be controlled by simply rubbing the creatures off between finger and thumb (again, impossible to do this with honeysuckles without damaging the flower buds) or by blasting them off the host plant with a jet of water.

Another sap-sucking insect is the capsid bug, a shy creature usually discovered through the damage it causes, for it kills the plant tissue it feeds on so the leaves become marked with little dead patches.

Caterpillars can eat considerable areas of leaf; pick them off by hand, or use a pesticide if there are many of them. Leafminers also eat leaves, but they live inside the leaf and chew the soft tissues between the upper and lower surfaces to leave pale traces of their passage. Again, there are pesticides that can deal with them.

Earwigs can be a problem, too. Roses may be invaded by the leaf-rolling rose sawfly, which rolls the leaves up tightly; if there are too many to pick off, you will need to use a systemic insecticide.

All these creatures affect mainly the leaves or flower buds of your climbers. Scale insects and froghoppers stick to the stems. Froghoppers protect themselves with the frothy coating known as cuckoospit; inside they are soft and vulnerable and can easily be squashed between unsqueamish fingers.

In cooler climates whitefly and red spider mite are chiefly a problem under glass. Whitefly, which are like tiny white moths, cause much the same damage as aphids and should be controlled by chemical pesticides or living predators. Red spider mite are most active in dry conditions, so you may be able to keep them under control by increasing the humidity. There are also chemical or biological controls available. Red spider mites are sap suckers, so tiny that they are usually not spotted until the gardener notices the mottled discoloration on the leaves they have infested.

One of the worst threats to young, soft growths is the slug. Slugs love damp weather and can make a meal of a delicate clematis shoot in minutes. The ultimate sanction of the heavy boot, or the old-fashioned remedy of a sprinkling of kitchen salt is still as good as any. For general protection rather than individual slug murder, you can put out saucers of beer or – shielding them from pets – use slug pellets. There are various 'green' slug controls available too.

Sometimes plants are damaged at soil level not by slugs, but by cutworms; use an insecticidal dust to control them.

PROPAGATION

After all these gloomy thoughts about what can damage or even kill your plants, it is pleasant to turn to ways of making more. Climbers can be propagated in the same ways as any other plant, though not all methods will suit every climber.

Nature's way is the seed. This is how to increase all annual and biennial climbers and many of the fast-growing perennials that we grow as annuals in climates colder than their own native lands: plants such as *Cobaea scandens*, *Eccremocarpus scaber* and the asarinas. Many woody climbers can also be raised from seed, though you may not get offspring exactly like the parent, especially if you have saved seed of a garden variety. Some even sow themselves: the apricot-coloured musk rose 'Treasure Trove' appeared as a chance seedling in John Treasure's garden near the Welsh borders in western England.

Very many climbers can be increased by cuttings. The most common method is to take half-ripe cuttings in summer. Many easy climbers, such as honeysuckles, can be struck from half-ripe cuttings set in sandy, well-drained soil in the open, thoroughly watered in and covered with a plastic cloche, shaded on hot days. You can also set them in pots or trays, in a frame or greenhouse, covering them with fine polythene film, or use a propagating case.

Propagating cases vary from the simple tray-plus-cover to something much more sophisticated. They can be good fun to play with, but most climbers will root perfectly well without such technology. Bottom heat, from a propagating case or from cables laid in a frame, is probably the most useful artificial aid and the first to go for if you are ambitious for more than just a pot on the windowsill.

The usual way to prepare a cutting is to trim it just below and just above a node or joint, but clematis cuttings are usually internodal, that is, you cut the stem between two joints, so each cutting has just one pair of buds. Species clematis, with the exception of some like the tricky *C. armandii*, are generally easy, and many of the large-flowered kinds can be rooted without difficulty too.

Many vines can be propagated by single bud cuttings taken from mature stems. They and many other climbers can also be increased by layering. If there is a convenient stem, still young but not soft and sappy, near the ground, conventional layering is the easier method. Make sure the soil mixture into which you peg the layered shoot is congenial; a cutting compost dug into the soil will help to encourage the new roots to grow.

Failing a convenient branch near ground level, air layering can often work well. Here the stem to be layered is wrapped in damp sphagnum moss and sealed in polythene. After the roots are well formed, the stem is severed just below the root mass and the new plant potted up to establish itself before planting out.

Some herbaceous climbers, such as the golden hop, can be simply increased by division or digging up rooted suckers, and some climbers such as *Campsis*, *Celastrus* and *Tropaeolum speciosum* can be increased by root cuttings.

Overleaf: One of the toughest climbers is Clematis montana, *willing to grow even in cold, dark places where its white flowers gleam from the shadows.*

A CALENDAR OF COLOUR FROM CLIMBERS AND WALL PLANTS

Winter-flowering climbers and wall plants

Acacia dealbata – small evergreen tree; fragrant yellow mimosa flowers

Azara microphylla – small evergreen tree/large shrub; tiny fragrant yellow flowers

Buddleja asiatica – large evergreen shrub; fragrant white flowers

Buddleja auriculata – large deciduous shrub; fragrant ivory flowers

Camellia sasanqua & cvs – medium-sized evergreen shrub; fragrant flowers, white, pink or crimson

Chimonanthus praecox & cvs – large deciduous shrub; very fragrant pale yellow flowers

Clematis cirrhosa – evergreen climber to 3 m (10 ft); flowers cream, often maroon-freckled

C. napaulensis – semi-evergreen climber to 6 m (20 ft); flowers creamy yellow

Daphne bholua & cvs – deciduous, semi-evergreen or evergreen shrub of medium size; fragrant flowers, white or pink from red-purple buds

D. odora & cvs – small evergreen shrub; fragrant pink-white flowers

Garrya elliptica & cvs – large evergreen shrub; long grey catkin-like tassels

Jasminum nudiflorum – large sprawling deciduous shrub; bright yellow flowers

Spring-flowering climbers and wall plants

Acacia baileyana – small evergreen tree; fragrant yellow flowers

A. pravissima – small evergreen tree; fragrant yellow flowers

Akebia quinata – deciduous climber to 9 m (30 ft); fragrant chocolate-maroon flowers

Azara dentata – large evergreen shrub; yellow flowers

A. lanceolata – large evergreen shrub; yellow flowers

Buddleja caryopteridifolia – medium-sized shrub; fragrant, lilac flowers spring or autumn

B. farreri – large deciduous shrub; fragrant lilac flowers

Camellia japonica & cvs – medium or large evergreen shrubs; flowers white, pink, red or striped, single or double

C. reticulata & cvs – large evergreen shrubs; flowers pink or red, semi-double or double

C. × williamsii & cvs – large evergreen shrubs; flowers white, pink or red, single or double

Cantua buxifolia – small evergreen shrub; cherry-red flowers

Ceanothus arboreus 'Trewithen Blue' – large evergreen shrub; bright blue flowers

C. 'Cascade' – medium-sized evergreen shrub; bright blue flowers

C. 'Concha' – medium-sized evergreen shrub; bright blue flowers

C. 'Delight' – medium-sized evergreen shrub; rich blue flowers

C. dentatus – medium-sized evergreen shrub; bright blue flowers

C. impressus – medium-sized evergreen shrub; bright blue flowers

C. 'Italian Skies' – medium-sized shrub; deep blue flowers

C. × *lobbianus* 'Southmead' – medium-sized evergreen shrub; bright blue flowers

C. papillosus roweanus – medium-sized evergreen shrub; deep blue flowers

C. 'Puget Blue' – medium-sized shrub; rich blue flowers

C. × *veitchianus* – medium-sized shrub; bright blue flowers

Chaenomeles, all – small to medium-sized deciduous shrubs; white, pink, orange or blood red flowers; some have large yellow aromatic fruits

Choisya ternata & cvs – medium-sized evergreen shrub; fragrant white flowers

C. 'Aztec Pearl' – medium-sized evergreen shrub; fragrant ivory flowers

Clematis alpina & cvs – deciduous climber to 2.5 m (8 ft); blue, white or dusky pink lantern flowers

C. armandii – evergreen climber to 6 m (20 ft); fragrant white or blush-pink flowers

C. forsteri – climber to 3 m (10 ft); fragrant lemon-green flowers

C. macropetala & cvs – deciduous climber to 3 m (10 ft); blue, white or dusky pink lantern flowers

C. montana & cvs – deciduous climber to 9 m (30 ft); white or pink flowers, sometimes fragrant

C. paniculata – evergreen climber to 4.5 m (15 ft); white flowers

Coronilla glauca & cvs – small evergreen shrub; fragrant

yellow pea flowers

C. valentina – dwarf evergreen shrub; fragrant yellow flowers

Cytisus monspessulanus – medium-sized semi-evergreen shrub; yellow pea flowers

C. 'Porlock' – large evergreen shrub; fragrant yellow flowers

C. proliferus – large deciduous shrub; white pea flowers

Drimys winteri – large evergreen shrub; white flowers

Forsythia suspensa & cvs – large deciduous shrub; yellow flowers

Genista monosperma – small deciduous shrub; white pea flowers

Holboellia coriacea – evergreen climber to 6 m (20 ft); very fragrant whitish flowers

H. latifolia – evergreen climber to 6 m (20 ft); very fragrant whitish flowers

Jasminum mesnyi – semi-evergreen climber to 6 m (20 ft); yellow semi-double flowers

Kerria japonica & cvs – small deciduous shrub; yellow flowers

Michelia doltsopa – small to medium-sized semi-evergreen tree; very fragrant white flowers

M. doltsopa 'Silver Cloud' – best form with golden-furred buds

M. figo – medium-sized evergreen shrub; very fragrant brown flowers

Olearia phlogopappa & cvs – small to medium-sized evergreen shrub; white, pink, mauve or violet daisy flowers

O. stellulata – small to medium-sized evergreen shrub; pure

white daisy flowers

Osmanthus delavayi – medium-sized evergreen shrub; very fragrant white flowers

Prostanthera 'Chelsea Pink' – small evergreen shrub; mauve-pink flowers

P. melissifolia – small evergreen shrub; mauve flowers

P. rotundifolia & cvs – small evergreen shrub; lilac or mauve-pink flowers

Prunus triloba – large deciduous shrub; bright pink flowers

Rhaphiolepis × *delacourii* & cvs – small to medium-sized evergreen shrub; rose-pink flowers

R. indica & cvs – small evergreen shrub; white flowers flushed pink

R. umbellata – small evergreen shrub; white flowers

Rosa banksiae & cvs – semi-evergreen climber to 7.5 m (25 ft); clustered ivory-white or soft yellow flowers, single or double

R. × *fortuneana* – deciduous climber to 7.5 m (25 ft); white double flowers

R. laevigata – semi-evergreen climber to 6 m (20 ft); fragrant white single flowers

R. 'Anemone' – semi-evergreen climber to 6 m (20 ft); clear pink single flowers

R. 'Ramona' – semi-evergreen climber to 6 m (20 ft); deep pink single flowers

Sophora macrocarpa – medium-sized evergreen shrub; rich yellow claw-like flowers

S. microphylla & cvs – small to large evergreen shrub; rich yellow claw-like flowers

S. tetraptera – small evergreen tree; rich yellow flowers

Stauntonia latifolia – evergreen climber to 9 m (30 ft); fragrant whitish flowers

Viburnum macrocephalum – medium-sized semi-evergreen shrub; white flowers in large domed heads

Early to midsummer-flowering climbers and wall plants

Abutilon ochsenii – medium-sized to large deciduous shrub; lavender-blue flowers

A. × suntense & cvs – large deciduous shrub; violet flowers

A. vitifolium & cvs – large deciduous shrub; pale to deep lavender or white flowers

Actinidia arguta – tall, vigorous deciduous climber; white flowers

Azara serrata – large deciduous shrub; yellow flowers

Bignonia capreolata – evergreen climber to 6 ft (20 ft); orange-red trumpet flowers

Buddleja colvilei & cvs – large deciduous shrub; large, tubular rose-red flowers

Ceanothus 'Autumnal Blue' – medium-sized evergreen shrub; deep rich blue flowers

C. 'Burkwoodii' – medium-sized evergreen shrub; rich blue flowers

Clematis, many large-flowered cvs – deciduous climbers reaching 2.5–4.5 m (8–15 ft); flowers single or double, white, mauve, lavender, blue, violet, purple or crimson

Clianthus puniceus & cvs – large semi-evergreen scrambling shrub; claw-like flowers, scarlet, shrimp pink or white

Cytisus battandieri – large deciduous shrub; pineapple-scented cones of yellow flowers

Decumaria barbara – semi-evergreen climber to 9 m (30 ft); fragrant white flowers

D. sinensis – evergreen climber to 4.5 m (15 ft); fragrant ivory flowers

Dendromecon rigida – large evergreen shrub; yellow poppy flowers

Fremontodendron 'Californian Glory' – large semi-evergreen shrub; cupped yellow flowers

F. californicum – large semi-evergreen shrub; cupped yellow flowers

F. mexicanum – large semi-evergreen shrub; cupped yellow flowers

Hebe 'Fairfieldiana' – small evergreen shrub; mauve flowers

H. 'Hagley Park' – dwarf evergreen shrub; pink-mauve flowers

H. hulkeana – small evergreen shrub; lilac flowers

Hydrangea petiolaris – deciduous climber to 18 m (60 ft); white lacecap flowers

Jasminum beesianum – deciduous climber to 3 m (10 ft); fragrant crimson flowers

J. polyanthum – evergreen climber to 7.5 m (25 ft); very fragrant white flowers from pink buds

J. × stephanense – deciduous

climber to 7.5 m (25 ft); fragrant pink flowers

Jovellana violacea – small evergreen shrub; pale lilac helmet flowers

Lonicera × americana (*L. × italica*) – deciduous climber to 9 m (30 ft); fragrant cream flowers from madder-pink buds

L. caprifolium – deciduous climber to 6 m (20 ft); very fragrant cream flowers

L. etrusca – deciduous or semi-evergreen climber to 9 m (30 ft); fragrant cream to yellow flowers

L. giraldii – evergreen climber to 6 m (20 ft) with velvety foliage; small purplish flowers

L. henryi – evergreen or semi-evergreen climber to 7.5 m (25 ft); small yellowish flowers

L. japonica & cvs – semi-evergreen climber to 9 m (30 ft); very fragrant white to yellow flowers

L. × tellmanniana – deciduous climber to 4.5 m (15 ft); coppery orange flowers

L. tragophylla – deciduous climber to 4.5 m (15 ft); long-tubed bright yellow flowers

Macfadyena unguis-cati – vigorous climber; bright yellow trumpet flowers

Melia azedarach – small deciduous tree; fragrant lilac flowers, long-lasting yellow fruits

Olearia frostii – small evergreen shrub; lilac daisy flowers

O. 'Henry Travers' (syn *O. semidentata*) – medium-sized shrub; large lavender, dark-eyed daisy flowers

Pittosporum tobira & cvs –

medium-sized to large evergreen shrub; very fragrant white flowers

Pyracantha, all – large evergreen shrubs; cream flowers

Robinia hispida – medium-sized to large deciduous shrub; pink pea flowers

Rosa, many rambling and musk roses – deciduous climbers from 4–9 m (13–30 ft); flowers white, pink, crimson, lilac-purple, yellow, etc.

Solanum crispum 'Glasnevin' – scrambling semi-evergreen shrub to 6 m (20 ft); violet flowers

Sutherlandia frutescens – medium-sized to large deciduous shrub; terracotta pea flowers

Vestia foetida – small evergreen shrub; tubular yellow flowers

Viburnum japonicum – large evergreen shrub; fragrant white flowers

Wisteria floribunda & cvs – deciduous climber to 6 m (20 ft); long tassels of lilac, pink or white fragrant flowers

W. sinensis & cvs – deciduous climber to 30 m (100 ft); tassels of lilac, pink or white fragrant flowers

W. venusta – deciduous climber to 9 m (30 ft); white flowers

High to late summer flowering climbers and wall plants

Abelia floribunda – medium-sized semi-evergreen shrub; cherry-magenta tubular flowers

Abutilon 'Kentish Belle' – small to medium-sized deciduous shrub; red and warm yellow bell flowers

A. megapotamicum – small to medium-sized deciduous shrub; waisted red and yellow flowers

Acca sellowiana – large evergreen shrub; pink and white flowers with crimson stamens

Aloysia triphylla – medium-sized deciduous shrub with lemon-scented leaves; tiny purple flowers

Araujia sericofera – evergreen climber to 6 m (20 ft); white or pink fragrant flowers

Asarina antirrhiniflora – herbaceous climber to 2 m (6 ft); red-purple foxglove flowers

A. barclayana – herbaceous climber to 3 m (10 ft); mauve-pink, purple or white flowers

A. erubescens – herbaceous climber to 2 m (6 ft); rose pink flowers

A. scandens – herbaceous climber to 3 m (6 ft); lavender flowers

Berberidopsis corallina – evergreen climber to 6 m (20 ft); blood red flowers

Bougainvillea, all – vigorous semi-evergreen or evergreen climbers; tiny flower surrounded by showy bracts, magenta, crimson, pink, salmon, scarlet, orange, yellow or white

Buddleja crispa – medium-sized to large deciduous shrub; fragrant lilac flowers

B. fallowiana 'Alba' – medium-sized to large deciduous shrub; ivory-white fragrant flowers

Bupleurum fruticosum – medium-

sized evergreen shrub; yellow-green flowers

Caesalpinia gilliesii – large deciduous shrub; bright yellow flowers with scarlet stamens

Calceolaria integrifolia – small evergreen shrub; yellow pouched flowers

C. 'Kentish Hero' – small evergreen shrub; rust-red pouched flowers

Callistemon citrinus 'Splendens' – large evergreen shrub; crimson bottlebrush flowers

C. linearis – large evergreen shrub; scarlet bottlebrush flowers

C. salignus – large evergreen shrub; pale yellow bottlebrush flowers

Calonyction aculeatum – herbaceous climber; large white flowers

Calystegia hederacea 'Flore Pleno' – herbaceous climber; double pink flowers

Campsis grandiflora – deciduous climber to 6 m (20 ft); orange-scarlet trumpet flowers

C. radicans – deciduous climber to 7.5 m (25 ft); orange-scarlet trumpet flowers

C. × *tagliabuana* 'Mme Galen' – deciduous climber to 6 m (20 ft); orange-scarlet trumpet flowers

Carpenteria californica – medium-sized evergreen shrub; white flowers

Cassia corymbosa – small deciduous shrub; yellow cupped flowers

Cestrum aurantiacum – medium-sized evergreen shrub; amber

yellow flowers

C. 'Newellii' – medium-sized evergreen shrub; scarlet flowers

C. roseum 'Ilnacullin' – medium-sized evergreen shrub; pink flowers

Clematis, many large-flowered cvs – deciduous climbers reaching 2.5–4.5 m (8–15 ft); flowers white, mauve, lavender, blue, violet, purple or crimson

C. campaniflora – deciduous climber to 6 m (20 ft); small blue-white flowers

C. texensis hybrids – deciduous or semi-herbaceous climbers to 3 m (10 ft); flowers pink or crimson, starry or tulip-shaped

C. viticella & hybrids – deciduous climbers to 3 m (10 ft); flowers white, mauve, violet, wine-red.

Cobaea scandens – annual/tender herbaceous climber; flowers purple or white cup-and-saucer

Convolvulus althaeoides – herbaceous climber; satiny pink flowers

C. cneorum – small evergreen silver-leaved shrub; white flowers from pink buds

C. elegantissimus – herbaceous climber; satiny pink flowers

Desfontainea spinosa – medium-sized evergreen shrub; tubular scarlet and yellow flowers

Dregea sinensis – deciduous climber to 3 m (10 ft); fragrant white flowers

Eccremocarpus scaber – annual/tender herbaceous climber; tubular flowers, orange, scarlet or amber-yellow

Escallonia bifida – large evergreen shrub; white flowers

Fallopia baldschuanica – deciduous climber to 12 m (40 ft); small pink-white flowers

Fuchsia 'Corallina' – deciduous shrub with semi-scandent stems; purple and red flowers

Grevillea 'Canberra Gem' – small evergreen shrub; crimson claw flowers

G. juniperina sulphurea – small evergreen shrub; pale yellow claw flowers

G. rosmarinifolia – small evergreen shrub; crimson claw flowers

Hydrangea serratifolia – evergreen climber to 9 m (30 ft); white flowers

Hypericum 'Rowallane' – small to medium-sized semi-evergreen shrub; yellow flowers

Ipomoea learii – climber to 12 m (40 ft); blue or violet flowers

I. nil – climber to 6 m (20 ft); purple, violet, blue, lavender or red flowers

I. tricolor 'Heavenly Blue' – annual/tender herbaceous climber; azure blue flowers

Itea ilicifolia – large evergreen shrub; creamy tassels

Jasminum grandiflorum – deciduous climber to 6 m (20 ft); very fragrant white flowers

J. officinale & cvs – deciduous climber to 6 m (20 ft); very fragrant white flowers

Lablab purpureus – annual climber; purple or white pea flowers

Lapageria rosea & cvs – evergreen climber to 4.5 m (15 ft); waxy rose pink or white bells

Lathyrus grandiflorus – herbaceous climber; large maroon and purple flowers

L. latifolius & cvs – herbaceous climber; rose-pink, clear pink or white flowers

L. nervosus – herbaceous climber; lavender-blue flowers

L. odoratus & cvs (sweet peas) – annual climber; fragrant flowers in many colours

L. rotundifolius – herbaceous climber; brick-pink flowers

L. tuberosus – herbaceous climber; clear pink flowers

L. × brownii 'Fuchsioides' – deciduous climber to 3 m (10 ft); vivid orange-scarlet scentless flowers

L. × brownii 'Dropmore Scarlet' – deciduous climber to 3 m (10 ft); vivid orange-scarlet scentless flowers

L. × heckrotii 'Gold Flame' – deciduous climber to 3 m (10 ft); orange-pink fragrant flowers

L. japonica & cvs – semi-evergreen climber to 9 m (30 ft); very fragrant white to yellow flowers

L. periclymenum & cvs – deciduous climber to 6 m (20 ft); cream and pink flowers

L. sempervirens – semi-evergreen climber to 9 m (30 ft); vivid scarlet flowers

Magnolia delavayi – large evergreen shrub or tree; very fragrant cream flowers

M. grandiflora & cvs – large evergreen shrub or tree; very fragrant ivory flowers

Mandevilla laxa – deciduous

climber to 4.5 m (15 ft); fragrant white flowers

Mimulus aurantiacus – small evergreen shrub; amber-orange flowers

M. longiflorus – small evergreen shrub; amber-yellow flowers

M. puniceus – small evergreen shrub; coppery crimson flowers

Mina lobata – annual/tender herbaceous climber; red flowers fading through orange to ivory

Mitraria coccinea – scrambling evergreen shrub to 3 m (10 ft); small scarlet trumpet flowers

Myrtus communis & cvs – large evergreen shrub; fragrant cream flowers

Pandorea jasminoides – evergreen climber to 3 m (10 ft); white, crimson-flecked trumpets

Passiflora antioquiensis – deciduous climber to 4.5 m (15 ft); long-tubed rich pink flowers

P. caerulea – evergreen climber to 9 m (30 ft); blue and white flowers

P. caerula 'Constance Elliott' – evergreen climber to 9 m (30 ft); white flowers

P. × caeruleoracemosa – evergreen climber to 9 m (30 ft); variable mauve-pink to lilac flowers

P. mollissima – evergreen climber to 10 m (30 ft); large white or mauve flowers

P. quadrangularis – climber to 9 m (30 ft); large white or mauve flowers

Pileostegia viburnoides – evergreen climber to 6 m (20 ft); frothy ivory flowers

Plumbago auriculata – scrambler to

4.5 m (15 ft); sky blue flowers

Podrania ricasoliana – evergreen or deciduous climber to 3 m (10 ft); pink trumpet flowers

Pueraria lobata – annual or herbaceous climber; purple pea flowers

Punica granatum & cvs – large deciduous shrub; scarlet, orange or white flowers, single or double

Rhodochiton atrosanguineum – herbaceous climber; maroon flowers with narrow black tube

Rosa, many large-flowered climbing and pillar – every colour except blue, on growth from 2.5 m (8 ft) to 6 m (20 ft)

Salvia greggii & cvs – small deciduous shrub; flowers magenta, crimson, peach

S. microphylla var. *neurepia* – small deciduous shrub; flowers scarlet

Schizophragma hydrangeoides – deciduous climber to 12 m (40 ft); white flowers with large cream bracts

S. integrifolium – deciduous climber to 12 m (40 ft); white flowers with large cream bracts

Solanum jasminoides 'Album' – semi-evergreen climber to 9 m (30 ft); white flowers

Sollya heterophylla – evergreen climber to 2 m (6 ft); pure blue flowers

S. parviflora – evergreen climber to 1.5 m (5 ft); deep blue flowers

Thunbergia alata – annual climber; yellow or orange, black-eyed flowers

Trachelospermum asiaticum – evergreen climber to 6 m (20 ft); fragrant white flowers

T. jasminoides & cvs – evergreen climber to 6 m (20 ft); fragrant white flowers

Tropaeolum peregrinum – annual climber; yellow flowers

T. speciosum – herbaceous climber; scarlet flowers

T. tuberosum – herbaceous climber; orange flowers

Tweedia caerulea – sub-shrubby climber; sky blue flowers

Autumn-flowering climbers and wall plants

Abutilon megapotamicum – small to medium-sized deciduous shrub; waisted red and yellow flowers

Aconitum volubile – herbaceous climber; slate blue helmet flowers

Campsis, all – deciduous climbers; orange-scarlet trumpet flowers

Ceanothus 'Autumnal Blue' – medium-sized evergreen shrub; blue flowers

C. 'Burkwoodii' – medium-sized evergreen shrub; blue flowers

Cestrum, all – deciduous shrubs; flowers red, amber, pink

Clematis, some large-flowered – flowers vary in colour

C. aethusifolia – deciduous climber to 3 m (10 ft); pale yellow bells

C. connata – deciduous climber to 6 m (20 ft); pale yellow bells

C. flammula – deciduous climber to 4.5 m (15 ft); white starry flowers

C. rehderiana – deciduous climber to 7.5 m (25 ft); pale yellow fragrant bells

C. serratifolia – deciduous climber to 3 m (10 ft); lemon yellow lanterns

C. tangutica & cvs – deciduous climber to 4.5 m (15 ft); yellow lanterns

C. tibetana & cvs – deciduous climber to 4.5 m (15 ft); yellow lanterns

Colquhounia coccinea – medium-sized deciduous shrub; orange-scarlet flowers

Eccremocarpus scaber – herbaceous climber; flowers orange etc.

Erythrina crista galli – large semi-herbaceous shrub; scarlet flowers

Escallonia bifida – large evergreen shrub; white flowers

Lapageria rosea & cvs – evergreen climber; rose or white flowers

Pileostegia viburnoides – evergreen climber to 6 m (20 ft); frothy ivory flowers

Rosa, many large-flowered climbers – various colours

Senecio scandens – semi-evergreen climber to 4.5 m (15 ft); yellow daisy flowers

Tropaeolum speciosum – herbaceous climber; scarlet flowers

T. tuberosum – herbaceous climber; orange flowers

APPENDIX II

CLIMBERS FOR AUTUMN AND WINTER LEAF COLOUR

Actinidia arguta – deciduous climber to 10 m (33 ft); yellow autumn foliage

Celastrus orbiculatus – deciduous climber to 12 m (40 ft); yellow autumn foliage

Parthenocissus henryana – deciduous climber to 6 m (20 ft); crimson autumn foliage

P. quinquefolia – deciduous climber to 12 m (40 ft); scarlet autumn foliage

P. tricuspidata – deciduous climber to 18 m (60 ft); scarlet autumn foliage

Vitis 'Brant' – deciduous climber to 9 m (30 ft); orange, scarlet and olive autumn colour

V. coignetiae – deciduous climber to 10 m (33 ft); purple, crimson and scarlet autumn colour

V. vinifera 'Purpurea' – deciduous climber to 6 m (20 ft); crimson autumn colour

CLIMBERS AND WALL SHRUBS FOR ORNAMENTAL FRUIT

Ampelopsis brevipedunculata – deciduous climber to 6 m (20 ft); porcelain-blue fruits

Billardiera longiflora – evergreen climber to 2 m (6 ft); royal blue fruits

Celastrus orbiculatus – deciduous climber to 12 m (40 ft); orange and yellow fruits

Clematis serratifolia – deciduous climber to 3 m (10 ft); silky white 'wigs'

C. tangutica – deciduous climber to 4.5 m (15 ft); silky white 'wigs'

C. tibetana – deciduous climber to 4.5 m (15 ft); silky white 'wigs'

Cotoneaster horizontalis – small spreading deciduous shrub; scarlet fruits

Pyracantha angustifolia – medium-sized evergreen shrub; orange fruits

P. atalantioides – large evergreen shrub; scarlet fruits

P. atalantioides 'Aurea' – large evergreen shrub; yellow fruits

P. coccinea 'Lalandei' – large evergreen shrub; orange-red fruits

P. 'Golden Charmer' – large evergreen shrub; yellow fruits

P. 'Mojave' – large evergreen shrub; red fruits

P. 'Navaho' – large evergreen shrub; red fruits

P. 'Orange Charmer' – large evergreen shrub; orange fruits

P. 'Orange Glow' – large evergreen shrub; orange fruits

P. 'Red Column' – large evergreen shrub; red fruits

P. rogersiana – large evergreen shrub; red fruits

P. rogersiana 'Flava' – large evergreen shrub; yellow fruits

P. 'Shawnee' – large evergreen shrub; amber-yellow fruits

P. 'Soleil d'Or' – large evergreen shrub; yellow fruits

P. 'Teton' – large evergreen shrub; yellow fruits

P. 'Watereri' – large evergreen shrub; red fruits

Rhaphithamnus spinosus – medium-sized to large evergreen shrub; deep blue fruits

Rosa, several musk roses – large deciduous climbers; orange to red fruits

Schisandra chinensis – deciduous climber to 9 m (30 ft); scarlet fruits

S. grandiflora – deciduous climber to 6 m (20 ft); scarlet fruits

S. rubriflora – deciduous climber to 6 m (20 ft); scarlet fruits

S. sphenanthera – deciduous climber to 7.5 m (25 ft); scarlet fruits

Vitis 'Brant' – deciduous climber to 9 m (30 ft); black grapes

APPENDIX IV

CLIMBERS WITH COLOURED OR VARIEGATED FOLIAGE

Actinidia kolomikta – deciduous climber to 6 m (20 ft); leaves green boldly marked pink and cream

Ampelopsis brevipedunculata 'Elegans' – deciduous climber to 3 m (10 ft); leaves splashed pink and cream

Euonymus fortunei, several – evergreen climbers to 3 m (10 ft); leaves variegated green and gold or green and white

Hedera colchica 'Dentata Variegata' – evergreen climber to 4.5 m (15 ft); leaves green edged primrose

H. colchica 'Sulphur Heart' – evergreen climber to 4.5 m (15 ft); leaves green with central primrose flash

H. helix, many – evergreen climbers, varying sizes and leaf shapes, variegation of many kinds

Humulus japonicus 'Variegatus' – annual climber, white-variegated leaves

H. lupulus 'Aureus' – herbaceous climber, yellow leaves

Jasminum officinale 'Argenteovariegatum' – deciduous climber to 6 m (20 ft); leaves white-variegated; fragrant white flowers

J. officinale 'Aureum' – deciduous climber to 6 m (20 ft); leaves yellow-variegated; fragrant white flowers

Lonicera japonica 'Aureo-reticulata' – semi-evergreen climber/scrambler to 3 m (10 ft); leaves gold-netted

Trachelospermum jasminoides 'Variegatum' – evergreen climber to 6 m (20 ft); leaves variegated cream on green, flushing pink and crimson in winter

Vitis vinifera 'Incana' – deciduous climber to 6 m (20 ft); leaves bloomed with grey

V. vinifera 'Purpurea' – deciduous climber to 6 m (20 ft); leaves purple, bloomed grey when young

CLIMBERS CLASSIFIED BY FLOWER COLOUR

Climbers with white or cream flowers

Actinidia arguta
A. deliciosa
Araujia sericofera
Bougainvillea, some
Calonyction aculeatum
Clematis alpina, several
C. armandii
C. flammula
C. macropetala 'Snowbird', 'White Swan'
C. montana, several
C. paniculata
Clematis, several large-flowered and viticella hybrids
Cobaea scandens 'Alba'
Decumaria barbara
D. sinensis
Dregea sinensis
Ercilla volubilis
Fallopia aubertii
F. baldschuanica
Hydrangea anomala petiolaris
H. serratifolia
Jasminum grandiflorum
J. officinale
J. polyanthum
Lapageria rosea 'Alba', 'White Cloud'
Lathyrus latifolius 'Albus', 'White Pearl'
Lonicera caprifolium
L. japonica
L. periclymenum 'Graham Thomas'
Mandevilla laxa
Passiflora caerulea 'Constance Elliott'
Pileostegia viburnoides
Rosa, many rambling and several large-flowered climbing
R. banksiae banksiae
R. bracteata
R. filipes 'Kiftsgate'
R. × fortuneana
R. gentiliana
R. helenae
R. laevigata
R. longicuspis
R. multiflora
Schizophragma hydrangeoides
S. integrifolium
Solanum jasminoides 'Album'
Trachelospermum asiaticum
T. jasminoides
Wisteria floribunda, some
W. sinensis, some
W. venusta

Climbers with yellow flowers

Bougainvillea, some
Campsis radicans 'Flava'
Clematis connata
C. rehderiana
C. serratifolia
C. tangutica
C. tibetana
Eccremocarpus scaber aurantiacus
Jasminum mesnyi
J. nudiflorum
Lonicera japonica
L. tragophylla
Macfadyena unguis-cati
Rosa, several large-flowered climbing and Noisette
R. banksiae 'Lutea'
R. 'Goldfinch' (rambler)
R. 'Mermaid'
Senecio scandens
Tropaeolum peregrinum

Climbers with orange to scarlet flowers

Bignonia capreolata
Bougainvillea, some
Campsis grandiflora
C. radicans
C. × tagliabuana 'Madame Galen'
Eccremocarpus scaber
Lonicera × brownii 'Dropmore Scarlet', 'Fuchsioides'
L. × heckrotti 'Gold Flame'
L. sempervirens

L. × *tellmanniana*
Mina lobata
Mitraria coccinea
Tropaeolum tuberosum

Climbers with crimson to magenta flowers

Berberidopsis corallina
Bougainvillea, several
Clematis, several large-flowered
   hybrids
C. texensis hybrids, some
C. viticella hybrids, some
Eccremocarpus scaber coccineus
Jasminum beesianum
Rosa, several rambling and
   large-flowered climbing
Tropaeolum speciosum

Climbers with maroon to purple flowers

Akebia quinata
Clematis viticella hybrids, some
Clematis, several large-flowered
   hybrids
Lablab purpureus
Lathyrus odoratus
Pueraria lobata
Rhodochiton atrosanguineum

Climbers with violet flowers

Cobaea scandens
Clematis, several large-flowered
   hybrids

Ipomoea learii
I. nil
Solanum crispum 'Glasnevin'
Wisteria × *formosa* 'Black Dragon'

Climbers with blue flowers

Clematis alpina, several
C. macropetala
Clematis, several large-flowered
   hybrids
Ipomoea learii
I. nil
I. tricolor 'Heavenly Blue'
Passiflora caerulea
Plumbago auriculata
Sollya heterophylla
S. parviflora
Tweedia caerulea

Climbers with mauve flowers

Aconitum volubile
Asarina scandens
Clematis campaniflora
Clematis, several large-flowered
   hybrids
Lathyrus nervosus
Passiflora × *caerulea-racemosa*
P. quadrangularis
Rosa, some rambling
Wisteria floribunda
W. sinensis

Climbers with pink or pink-effect flowers

Asarina antirrhiniflora
A. barclayana
A. erubescens
Bougainvillea, some
Calystegia hederacea 'Flore Pleno'
Clematis, several large-flowered
   hybrids
C. alpina, some
C. armandii 'Apple Blossom'
C. macropetala 'Markham's Pink'
Clematis texensis hybrids, some
C. montana rubens & forms
Convolvulus althaeoides
C. elegantissimus
Jasminum × *stephanense*
Lapageria rosea
Lathyrus grandiflorus
L. latifolius
L. rotundifolius
L. tuberosus
Lonicera periclymenum 'Belgica',
   'Serotina'
Pandorea jasminoides
Passiflora antioquiensis
P. mollissima
Podranea ricasoliana
R. 'Anemone'
R. 'Ramona'
Rosa, several rambling and
   large-flowered climbing
   hybrids
Rosa, Bourbon, several
Schizophragma hydrangeoides
   'Roseum'
Wisteria floribunda, some

WALL PLANTS CLASSIFIED BY FLOWER COLOUR

Wall shrubs with white or cream flowers

Abutilon × hybridum 'Boule de Neige'
A. vitifolium 'Veronica Tennant White'
Buddleja asiatica
B. auriculata
B. fallowiana 'Alba'
Camellia japonica, several
C. sasanqua 'Narumigata'
Carpenteria californica
Chaenomeles, some
Choisya 'Aztec Pearl'
C. ternata
Convolvulus cneorum
Cytisus proliferus
Drimys winteri
Escallonia bifida
Genista monosperma
Itea ilicifolia (greenish white)
Magnolia delavayi
M. grandiflora
Michelia doltsopa
Myrtus communis
Olearia phlogopappa
Osmanthus delavayi
Pittosporum tobira
Pyracantha, all
Viburnum japonicum
V. macrocephalum

Wall shrubs with yellow flowers

Abutilon × hybridum, some
Acacia baileyana
A. dealbata
A. pravissima
Azara dentata
A. lanceolata
A. microphylla
A. serrata
Bupleurum fruticosum
Caesalpinia gilliesii
Calceolaria integrifolia
Callistemon salignus
Cassia corymbosa
Chimonanthus praecox
Coronilla glauca
C. valentina
Cytisus battandieri
C. monspessulanus
C. 'Porlock'
Dendromecon rigida
Forsythia suspensa
Fremontodendron 'Californian Glory'
F. californicum
F. mexicanum
Grevillea juniperina sulphurea
Hypericum 'Rowallane'
Kerria japonica
Sophora macrocarpa

S. microphylla
S. tetraptera
Vestia foetida

Wall shrubs with orange to scarlet flowers

Abutilon megapotamicum & hybrids
Calceolaria 'Kentish Hero'
Chaenomeles, several
Cestrum aurantiacum
C. 'Newellii'
Clianthus puniceus
Desfontainea spinosa
Mimulus aurantiacus
M. longiflorus
Punica granatum
Salvia microphylla neurepia
Sutherlandia frutescens

Wall shrubs with crimson to magenta flowers

Abelia floribunda
Abutilon × hybridum 'Nabob'
Buddleja colvilei 'Kewensis'
Camellia japonica, several
C. sasanqua 'Crimson King'
Cantua buxifolia
Cestrum elegans
Fuchsia 'Corallina'
Grevillea 'Canberra Gem'

G. rosmarinifolia
Mimulus puniceus
Ribes speciosum
Salvia greggii
S. microphylla

Wall shrubs with purple to violet flowers

Abutilon ochsenii
A × suntense

Wall shrubs with blue flowers

Ceanothus arboreus 'Trewithen Blue'
C. 'Autumnal Blue'
C. 'Burkwoodii'
C. 'Cascade'
C. 'Concha'
C. 'Delight'
C. dentatus
C. impressus
C. 'Italian Skies'

C. × lobbianus 'Southmead'
C. papillosus roweanus
C. 'Puget Blue'
C. × veitchianus
Olearia phlogopappa 'Comber's Blue'
O. stellulata 'Master Michael'

Wall shrubs with mauve flowers

Abutilon vitifolium
Aloysia triphylla
Buddleja caryopteridifolia
B. crispa
B. farreri
Hebe 'Fairfieldiana'
H. hulkeana
Jovellana violacea
Melia azedarach
Olearia frostii
O. 'Henry Travers'
Prostanthera melissifolia
P. rotundifolia

Wall shrubs with pink flowers

Acca sellowiana
Buddleja colvilei
Camellia japonica, many
C. sasanqua
C. reticulata
C. × williamsii & hybrids
Cestrum roseum 'Ilnacullin'
Chaenomeles, some
Daphne bholua
D. odora
Hebe 'Hagley Park'
Olearia phlogopappa 'Comber's Pink'
Prostanthera 'Chelsea Pink'
P. rotundifolia rosea
Prunus triloba
Rhaphiolepis × delacourii
R. indica
R. umbellata
Robinia hispida
Salvia greggii 'Peach'

BIBLIOGRAPHY

Bean, W. J., *Trees and Shrubs Hardy in the British Isles* 4 vols., 8th (revised) ed. John Murray, 1976–80; supplement to 8th ed. John Murray, 1988.

——*Wall Shrubs and Hardy Climbers*, Putnam, 1939.

Beckett, Kenneth A., *Climbing Plants*, Croom Helm, 1983.

Fisk, J., *Clematis, the Queen of Climbers*, Cassell, 1989.

Fretwell, B., *Clematis*, Collins, 1989.

Grey-Wilson, Christopher & Matthews, Victoria, *Gardening on Walls*, Collins, 1983.

Haworth-Booth, M., *The Hydrangeas*, Garden Book Club, 1975.

Hilliers' Manual of Trees & Shrubs, David & Charles, 1972.

Lloyd, Christopher & Bennett, T. H., *Clematis*, Viking, 1989.

Lucas Phillips, C. E., *Climbing Plants for Walls & Gardens*, Heinemann, 1967.

Rose, P. Q., *Climbers & Wall Plants*, Blandford, 1982.

—— *Ivies*, Blandford Press, 1980.

Taylor, J. *Collecting Garden Plants*, Dent, 1988.

—— *Creative Planting with Climbers*, Ward Lock, 1991.

—— *Gardening in Shade*, Dent, 1991.

—— *Climbing Plants* (Kew Gardening Guides), Collingridge, 1987.

—— *The Milder Garden*, Dent, 1990.

Thomas, G. S., *Climbing Roses Old & New* rev. ed., Dent, 1978.

Vanderplank, J., *Passion Flowers*, Cassell, 1991.

INDEX

Page numbers in *italics* indicate an illustration which may appear on a different page to its text.

Abelia floribunda, 77, 114, 123
Abutilon, 85
    A. × *hybridum*, 123
    A. megapotamicum, 73, 76, 85, 114, 116, 123
    A. ochsenii, 56, 113, 124
    A. × *suntense*, 56, 113, 124
    A. vitifolium, *55*, 56, 113, 123, 124
Acacia baileyana, 28, 111, 123
    A. dealbata, 16–17, 111, 123
    A. pravissima, 28, 111, 123
Acca sellowiana, 77, 114, 124
Aconitum volubile, 85, 88, 116, 122
Actinidia arguta, 50, 113, 118, 121
    A. deliciosa, 50, 120
    A. kolomikta, 50, 120
    pruning, *100*
Air layering, 109
Akebia quinata, 20–21, 111, 122
Aloysia triphylla, 81, 114, 124
Ampeloposis brevipeunduculata, 61, 88, 119, 120
Aphids, 108
Araujia sericofera, 78, 114, 120
Arches, 37–38
Asarina, 60–61
    A. antirriniflora, 61, 114, 122
    A. barclayana, 56, 61, 114, 122
    A. erubescens, 61, 114, 122
    A. scandens, 61, 114, 122
Autumn plants, 82–92, 118
Azara dentata, 29, 111, 123
    A. lanceolata, 29, 111, 123
    A. microphylla, 16, 29, 77, 111, 123
    A. serrata, 29, 113, 123

Berberis darwinii, 36
Berberidopsis corallina, 71, 114, 122
Berries, plants for, 88–89
Bigonia capreolata, 53, 113, 121
Billardiera longiflora, 88, 119
Blue flowering plants, 122, 124
Botrytis, 106

Bougainvillea, 114, 121, 122
Buddleja asiatica, 17, 111, 123
    B. auriculata, 17, 111, 123
    B. caryopteridifolia, 32, 111, 124
    B. colvilei, 55, 113, 123, 124
    B. crispa, 76, 114, 124
    B. fallowiana, 81, 114, 123
    B. farreri, 32, 111, 124
Bupleurum fruticosum, 77, 114, 123

Caesalpina gilliesii, 77, 114, 123
Calceolaria integrifolia, 76, 114, 123
    C. 'Kentish Hero', 76, 114, 123
Callistemon citrinus 'Splendens', 77, 114
    C. linearis, 77, 114
    C. salignus, 77, 114, 123
Calonyction aculeatum, 81, 114, 121
Calystegia hederacea, 61, 114, 122
Camellia, 24–25
    C. japonica, 14, 24, 111, 123, 124
    C. reticulata, 24, 111, 124
    C. sasanqua, 14, 24, 111, 123, 124
    C. × *williamsii*, 25, 111, 124
Campsis, 80, 85, 116
    cuttings, 109
    C. grandiflora, 80, 114, 121
    pruning, *100*
    C. radicans, 80, 114, 121
    C. × *tagliabuana*, 80, 114, 122
Cantua buxifolia, 32, *33*, 111, 124
Capsid bugs, 108
Carpentaria californica, 81, 114, 123
Cassia corymbosa, 77, 114, 123
Caterpillars, 108
Ceanothus, 35, 113, 124
    C. arboreus, 25, 111, 124
    C. 'Burkwoodii', 53, 116, 124
    C. dentatus, 25, 111, 124
    C. impressus, 25, 111, 124
    C. × *lobbianus*, 25, 112, 124
    C. papillosus roweanus, 27, 112, 124
    C. × *veitchianus*, 25, 112, 124
Celastrus orbiculatus, 89, 118, 119
    cuttings, 109

Cestrum aurantiacum, 74, 114, 123
    C. elegans, 124
    C. 'Newellii', 77, 115, 123
    C. roseum 'Ilnacullin', 77, 115, 124
Chaenomeles, 112, 123, 124
Chaemonanthus praecox, 16, 123
    Ch. speciosa, 20
    Ch. × *superba*, 20
Chimonanthus praecox, 111
Choisya 'Aztec Pearl', 23, 24, 123
    Ch. ternata, 12, 23, 85, 112, 123
Clematis, 44–49, 78, 86, 113, 115, 116
    C. aethusifolia, 84, 116
    C. alpina, 20, 23, 35, 36, 112, 121, 122
    C. armandii, 32–33, 112, 121, 122
    C. campaniflora, 67, 115, 122
    C. cirrhosa, 17, 111
    C.c. balearica, 7, 17
    C. connata, 84, 116, 121
    cuttings, 109
    C. flammula, *82*, 84, 116, 121
    C. forsteri, 33, 112
    C. indivisa, *23*, 33
    large-flowered, 64–68, 82, 121, 122
    C. macropetala, 20–21, 112, 121, 122
    C. montana, 18–19, *29*, 35, 80, 112, 121
    C.m. rubens, 19–20, 122
    C.m. sericea, 20
    C. napaulensis, 111
    orange peel, 82
    C. orientalis see *C. tibetana*
    C. paniculata, 112, 121
    pruning, *100*, 101
    C. rehderiana, 84, 117, 121
    C. serratifolia, 84, 117, 119, 121
    C. tangutica, 84, 117, 119, 121
    C. texensis, 68, 115, 122
    C. tibetana, 84, 117, 119, 121
    C. viticella, 36, 66–67, 115, 121, 122
    C. wilsonii, 20
Clianthus puniceus, 54, 113, 123
Cobaea scandens, 34, 64, 115, 121, 122

Cold wall plants, 18–21
Colquhounia coccinea, 85, 117
Compost, 93–94
Convolvulus althaeoides, 61, 115, 122
    C. cneorum, 76, 115, 123
    C. elegantissimus, 61, 115, 122
Coronilla glauca, 112, 123
    C. valentina, 112, 123
Cotoneaster horizontalis, 17, 89, 119
Cuttings, 109
Cytisus battandieri, 54, 113, 123
    C. canariensis, 28–29
    C. monspessulanus, 29, 112, 123
    C. 'Porlock', 112, 123
    C. proliferus, 29, 112, 123

Daphne bholua, 16, 111, 124
    D. odora, 16, 111, 124
Decumaria barbara, 16, 111, 124
    D. sinensis, 12, 58, 113, 121
Dendromecon rigida, 53, 113, 123
Desfontainea spinosa, 69, 71, 115, 123
Diseases, 106–8
Division, 109
Dregea sinensis, 76, 115, 121
Drimys winteri, 29, 112, 123

Earwigs, 108
Eccremocarpus scaber, 36, 54, 64, 115, 117, 121, 122
Elaeagnus pungens, 47
Ercilla volubilis, 121
Eriobotrya japonica, 12, *13*
Erythrina crista-galli, 85, 117
Escallonia 'Apple Blossom', 88
    E. bifida, 77, *85*, 115, 117, 123
Euonymus fortunei, 9, *11*, 120
Evergreen foliage plants, 8–13

Fallopia aubertii, 121
    F. baldschuanica, 52, 115
Fatsia japonica, 12, *13*
Feijoa see Acca
Fences, 105
Fertilizers, 97
Foliage plants, 90–92, 120
Forsythia × intermedia, 21
    F. suspensa, 21, *23*, 112, 123
Fremontodendron 'Californian Glory', *54*, 113, 123
    F. californicum, 53, 113, 123
    F. mexicanum, 53, 113, 123
Froghoppers, 108
Fruits, plants for, 88–89, 119
Fuchsia 'Corallina', 76, 115, 124

Garrya elliptica, 12, *14*, 111
    G. × thuretii, 12
Genista monosperma, 29, 112, 123
Grevillea 'Canberra Gem', 115, 124
    G. juniperina var. *sulphurea*, 76, 115, 123
    G. rosmarinifolia, 76, 115, 124
Grey mould, 106

Hebe 'Fairfieldiana', 124
    H. 'Hagley Park', 124
    H. Hulkeana, 57, 113, 124
Hedera colchica, 12, 92, 120
    H. helix, 120
High wall climbers, 77–79
Holborllis, 12
    H. coriacea, 34, 112
    H. latifolia, 33–34, 112
Honey fungus, 106
Humulus japonicus 'Variegatus', 62, 120
    H. lupulus 'Aureus', 52, 120
Hydrangea, 9
    H. anomola petiolaris, 52, 121
    H. petiolaris, 69, 113
    pruning, *100*
    H. serratifolia, 69, 115, 121
Hypericum 'Rowallane', 77, 115, 123

Ipomoea learii, 60, 115, 122
    I. nil, 115, 122
    I. tricolor, 60, 122
Itea ilicifolia, 77, 115, 123

Jasminum beesianum, 53, 113, 122
    J. grandiflorum, 80, 115, 121
    J. mesnyi, 33, 112, 121
    J. nudiflorum, 17, 111, 121
    J. officinale, 80, 115, 120, 121
    J. polyanthum, 57–58, 113, 121
    J. × stephanense, 53, 113, 122
Jovellana violacea, 57, 113, 124

Kerria japonica, 21, 112, 123

Lablab purpureus, 60, 115, 122
Lapageria rosea, 71, *72*, 115, 117, 121, 122
Lathyrus grandiflorus, 60, 115, 122
    L. latifolius, 59, *62*, 115, 121, 122
    L. nervosus, 115, 122
    L. odoratus, 59, 115, 122
    L. rotundifolius, 60, 115, 122
    L. tuberosus, 60, 115, 122
Leafminers, 108
Lonicera, *46*, 122
    L. × americana, 50, 68, 113

L. × brownii, 68, 122
L. caprifolium, 50, 68, 113, 121
L. etrusca, 50, 113
L. giraldii, 12, 113
L. heckrottii 'Gold Flame', 68, 122
L. henryi, 12, 113
L. japonica, 12, 50, 113, 120, 121
L. periclymenum, 68, 121, 122
L. sempervirens, 68, 122
L. × tellmanniana, 54, 69, 74, 113, 122
L. tragonphylla, 54, 69, 113, 121

Macfadyena unguis-cati, *52*, 53, 113, 121
Magnolia, 29
    M. delavayi, 81, 123
    M. grandiflora, 81, 115, 123
Mahonia aquifolium, 17
Mandevilla laxa, 78, 79, 115, 121
Mauve flowering plants, 122, 124
Melia azedarach, 56–57, 113, 124
Michelia doltsopa, 29, 32, 112, 123
    M. figo, 32, 112
Mimulus aurantiacus, 76, 115, 123
    M. longiflorus, 76, 116, 123
    M. puniceus, 76, 116, 124
Mina lobata, 76, 116, 122
Mitraria coccinea, 71, 116, 122
Mulch, 98
Myrtus communis, 80, 116, 123

Olearia frostii, 57, *58*, 113, 124
    O. phlogopappa, 32, 112, 123, 124
    O. semidentata, 57
    O. stellulata, 27, 32, 112, 124
Orange flowering plants, 121–2, 123
Osmanthus delavayi, 19, 23, 112, 123

Paeonia lutea ludlowii, 35
Pandorea jasminoides, 80, 116, 122
Parthenocissus henryana, 91, 92, 118
    P. quinquefolia, 90–91, 118
    P. tricuspidata, 118
    P.t. 'Veitchii', 91
Passiflora antioquiensis, 80, 116, 122
    P. caerulea, 79, 116, 121, 122
    P. × caeruleo-racemosa, 78, 116, 122
    P. mollissima, 80, 116, 122
    P. quadrangularis, 78, 116, 122
Perfumed plants, 14–17, 57–58, 79–81
Pergolas, 37–38
Pests, 108
Physocarpus opulifolius, 35
Pieris formosa forrestii, 35
Pileostgeia viburnoides, 9, 12, 69, 116, 117, 121

Pink flowering plants, 122
Pittosporum tenuifolium, 21
    P. tobira, 58, 113, 123
Planting up, 96–97
Plumbago auriculata, 77, 116, 122
Podrania ricasoliana, 80, 116, 122
Polygonum see Fallopia
Powdery mildew, 106
Propagation, 109
Prostanthera melissifolia, 112, 124
    P.m. var. *parvifolia*, 32
    P. rotundifolia, 32, 112, 124
Pruning, 99–103
Prunus triloba, 29, 112, 124
Pueraria lobata, 60, 116, 122
Punica granatum nana, 76, 123
Purple flowering plants, 122, *124*
Pyracantha, 9, 58, 88–89, 114, 119, 123
    P. angustifolia, 89, 119
    P. atalantioides, 89, 119
    P. coccinea, 119
    P. rogersiana, 89, 119

Red flowering plants, 121–2, 123–4
Red spider mite, 108
Rhaphiolepsis × *delacourii*, 32, 112, 124
    Rh. indica, 112, 124
    Rh. umbellata, 112, 124
Rhaphithamnus spinosus, 88, *119*
Rhodochiton astrosangineum, 56, 61, 62, 66, 116, 122
Ribes speciosum, 32, 112, 124
Robinia hispida, 54, 114, 124
Rope swags, 37–38
Rosa banksiae, 34, 35, 112, 121
    R. bracteata, 81, 121
    R. filipes, 44, 121
    R. × *fortuneana*, 34, 112, 121
    R. gentiliana, 42, 89, 121
    R. helenae, 42, 89, 121
    R. leavigata, 34, 112, 121
    R. longicuspis, 42, 44, *89*, 121

R. moyesii, 84
R. multiflora, 42, 44, 89, 121
Roses, *46*, 114, 116, 117, 121
    bourbon, 71
    musk, *39*, 119
    Noisette, 72, 121
    pillar, 65–66
    pruning, 101–2
    rambling, 40–44, 121, 122

Salvia greggii, 76, 116, 124
    S. microphylla, 76, 124
    S.m. neurepia, 123
Sawflies, 108
Scale insects, 108
Schisandra chinensis, 119
    S. grandiflora, 119
    S. rubriflora, 89, 119
    S. sphenanthera, 119
Schizophragma hydrangeoides, 69, 116, 121, 122
    S. integrifolium, 69, 116, 121
Seeds, 109
Senecio scandens, 84, *86*, 117, 121
Shade plants, 69
Sheltered places plants, 21–34
Silverleaf, 106
Skimmia japonica, 12–13
    S. × *confusa*, 13
Slugs, 108
Soil preparation, 93–95
Solanum crispum 'Glasnevin', 56, 114
    S. jasminoides 'Album', 78, 116, 121
Sollya heterophylla, 76, 116, 122
    S. parviflora, 76, 116, 122
Sophora macrocarpa, 27, 112, 123
    S. microphylla, 27, *28*, 112, 123
    S. tetraptera, 27, 113, 123
Spring plants, 18–36
Stauntonia hexaphylla, 12, 34
    S. latifolia, 113
Summer plants, 37–82

Support, 103–6
Sutherlandia frutescens, 54, 114, 123

Tender shrubs, 76–77
Trachelospermum asiaticum, 79, 116, 121
    T. jasminoides, 9, *11*, 78, 116, 120, 121
Trellis, 37–38, 104–5
Tropaeolum majus, 60
    T. peregrinum, 60, 116, 121
    T. speciosum, 60, 69, 85, 116, 117, 122
        cuttings, 109
    T. tuberosum, 60, 85, *94*, 116, 117, 122
Tweedia caerulea, 76, 116, 122

Vestia foetida, 54, 114, 123
Viburnum japonicum, 12, 58, 114, 123
    V. macrocephalum, 27, 29, 113, 123
Vine eyes, 104
Vitis 'Brant', 88, *90*, 92, 118, 119
    V. coignetiae, 92, *98*, 118
        pruning, *100*
        cuttings, 109
    V. vinifera, 41
    V.v. 'Incana', 120
    V.v. 'Purpurea', 78, 88, 92, 118, 120

Warm places, plants for, 85–88
    wall plants, 21–34
Watering, 96
White flowering plants, 121, 123
Whitefly, 108
Wilt, 106
Winter plants, 8–17
Winter protection, 97–98
Wisteria, 38–40
    W. floribunda, 39, 40, 114, 121, 122
        pruning, 102–3
    W. sinensis, 39, 40, 114, 121, 122
    W. venusta, 40, 114, 121

Yellow flowering plants, 121, 123